Table of Contents

Author's note: 3
London: A brief History 4
London Today: An Overview 10
    The People of London – Demographics 10
    Local customs and etiquette 10
    Weather 14
    More important considerations 15
Getting to London 18
    Flying 18
    Rail to London 26
    Ferry Services 29
Transport in London 30
    Driving 30
    Public Transport – The Oyster Card 33
    Journey Planning 36
    London Underground 37
    Buses 40
    Cycling 44
At a Glance: Top 10 Must-See Attractions 51
Neighbourhood Guides: London Area by Area 62
    Westminster, Victoria & St. James's 64
    The Southbank 81
    West End and Trafalgar Square 89
    Kensington & The Museums 106
    The City 117
    London Bridge 131
    Hyde Park, Notting Hill & Bayswater 140
    Marylebone, Bloomsbury and Camden 146
    Further Afield 158
Shopping 169
Music, Arts and Nightlife 180
    Musicals 180
    Plays 185
    Dance, Opera and Other Performances 186

Music and Arts: 188

Nightlife 193

Sport 197

Dining 204
Afternoon Tea 204
Luxury Dining 207
Affordable Dining 209

Saving Money in London 211

2016 Seasonal Events 216

A Special Thanks! 227

Author's note:

Hello, welcome, and congratulations on purchasing *The Independent Guide to London 2016*.

My name is John Coast, and I was born and raised a Londoner. Despite having travelled around the world, and having held jobs and lived in places across Europe and the US, for me there is still no city around the world that can match the allure of London. Whether it is the historic streets of the City of London where the romans founded Londinium, the skyscrapers that scream money and finance, the plays and musicals in Theatreland, or the serenity of the capital's many parks, every corner of London holds a surprise.

From a very young age I knew that London was unlike any other city. No matter what location I visited around the world, I couldn't help but compare it to London. This became even more evident as I worked my first ever job as a tour guide on an open-top London bus. Here I would recount bloody stories from London's past, and marvel visitors with the city's architecture as we made our way round central London's streets in two-and-a-half hours.

It was while working as a tour guide that the idea for this travel guide first came about. I wanted to be able to share London with people worldwide.

Having picked up travel guides for various cities around the world, I always found that they included information that simply wasn't necessary, whilst missing things that I *did* want to know. I always figured that travelers would want to know about the following things before arrival: how do I get to London *and* around London, what are the top sites, good places to eat, good places to shop, where is the theatre district and what is good to see, the people and their customs, a bit of history and some tips from a local. If that's what you want from a travel guide, then this is the guide for you! If you want a listing of every shop and restaurant in every area in a heavy book for you to lug around, then this is *not* the guide for you.

This guide is designed to be an easy read that you can reference before, during and after your trip. While visiting London, I recommend you have a city map and an Underground map with you, as well as this travel guide.

Happy reading and enjoy your trip to London. I'm sure you'll fall in love with the city and will want to come back many more times!

-- John Coast

London: A brief History

London is one of the most beautiful and culturally diverse places in the world with the world's fifth largest economy. The city has changed through centuries of ups and downs to become the magnificent city that it is today. This section takes a brief and interesting look at London's history.

The City is Built & Burned ~ Roman London (43 to 410 AD)

Today's London started off as a civilian town called Londinium, established by the Romans a few years after the invasion of AD43. Londinium is believed to have been equivalent to the size of Hyde Park today, and the Roman army built a sturdy wooden bridge over the Thames, east of where today's London Bridge is situated. As a result of the bridge and construction of roads from the Londinium port, there was an influx of merchants, traders and other urban dwellers in search of better living conditions and opportunities.

Over the next few years, Londinium prospered and became an important town but this came to a halt when in 60AD, Queen Boudicca, of the Icene tribe of Norfolk, targeted Londinium as a show of her antagonism of Roman rule. Boudicca and her army razed Londinium to the ground, killing thousands in the process, and as a result orchestrated one of the first recorded burnings of London in history. The buildings at the time were made of wood and clay and therefore burnt very easily.

After the invasion of Boudicca, it did not take long for the Romans to re-establish control. The strategic location of Londinium made it too valuable to forfeit, therefore it was hastily rebuilt. It became a walled and planned Roman city. The rebirth was the beginning of a golden era of trade and by 100AD, large amounts of goods were being traded in Londinium – emanating from, and going to, extensive corners of the empire.

Luxury goods such as pottery, wine, olive oil, marble and slaves became rampant in Londinium through import from Spain, Italy, Gaul and Greece, while a viable export market for tin, silver, copper, oysters, corn and woolen cloak was established.

London's Fortune Changes ~ End of Roman London

Londinium boasted an amphitheatre, a temple, a palace, bath houses and a large fort at its peak but as the proverb says "every beginning must have an end". During the visit of Emperor Hadrian in 122AD, it was estimated that Londinium had a population of about 45,000 and was largely perceived as a cultural melting point, due to its cosmopolitan mix. However, by the 3rd century, Londinium's fortunes began to change as a result of several factors, including: political instability in the empire, recession, as well as barbarian and pirate attacks.

Over the next century, soldiers were constantly pegged away from Britannia to deal with barbarian attacks elsewhere and Emperor Constantine II recalled the last troops in 407 AD. A few years later, Emperor Honorius declined requests from Britain for military aid and this officially marked the end of Roman rule, thereby setting in motion the end of Roman London. By the middle of the 5th century, Londinium was completely deserted and abandoned.

The Viking Invasion of London

When the Romans left, London ceased to be an important town and it fell into obscurity. But the location of London on the Thames was an important factor, so the 7th century witnessed trade expand and the city flourished once more. The growth was stable and free flowing, so as a result, by the 9th century, London became a prosperous trading center and its affluence attracted the attention of the Danish Vikings. The Vikings were severe: in 851 the Danes attacked and destroyed the city.

The tenth century is a confusing one for historians, but it is believed that the English, Danish and then Norman kings had control of the city at different times.

By 1014, while the Danish were controlling the city, a large force of Norwegian Vikings and Anglo-Saxons attacked London, which led to the fall of the London Bridge – this is still a popular, and well-known, nursery rhyme today.

When Danish King Cnut ascended to power in 1017, attacks ceased due to Cnut's willingness to unite Anglo-Saxons with the Danes and the invitation of Danish merchants to settle in the city. Until King Cnut's death, London prospered but his demise reverted the city back to Anglo-Saxons rule under Edward the Confessor.

London became the largest city in England and the most prosperous in Britain, but it was not the capital of the realm. Winchester held that role until the 12th century.

Disaster ~ The Great Plague and the Great Fire of London

By the 1600s, the growth and continued expansion of London led to the influx of all classes of people and there were a large number of people who lived in extreme poverty in the city. Poverty became so rife that city sanitation was adversely affected as people disposed of their waste (both organic and human) out in the streets of the city and as a consequence, London became filthy and infested with rats and fleas.

In 1665, the early victims of The Great Plague were first discovered in the poorer areas of London due to the deplorable living conditions. The spread of the plague was aided by the overpopulation of the area, which encouraged close contact between healthy and infected people, and even contact with rats and fleas. The disease spread so quickly that the rich relocated to the countryside for safety while the poor had no other choice than to stay put.

As a response to the disease, some new laws were created to help curb the spread of the plague: sending of the military to guard certain areas, painting red crosses on doors of the infected, the killing of dogs, and searchers who hunted down dead bodies for mass burials etc. The climax of the plague was in September 1665 when the summer heat peaked. The next winter halted the spread of the plague as the cold took its toll on the rats and fleas.

Though the real tragedy had passed by the tail end of 1665, the demise of the disease was in part due to the Great Fire of London in 1666. The fire destroyed the infested areas where rats had multiplied. The fire was reported to have burnt down over 13,000 houses, 88 parish churches, and left over 70,000 inhabitants of London homeless. Only 6 people were reported to be killed by the fire which lasted from the 2nd to 5th September 1666.

The rebuilding of the city after The Great Fire was swift; King Charles appointed commissioners including Christopher Wren to supervise the rebuilding. The supervisors were tasked with the duty of determining the length of streets, quality of materials and positioning of important public structures like markets, churches, and secular buildings. Wren's grand plan for London was never used, but, nevertheless, by the end of 1670, over 6000 houses had been built.

Christopher Wren, who was knighted in 1673, supervised the construction of fifty-one parish churches and started the construction of St Paul's Cathedral. Another notable name in the rebuilding of London is John Nash, who designed Buckingham Palace and Regent Street, as well as Marble Arch in 1827, to be the official pathway to the Cour d'Honneur of Buckingham Palace.

The Bank of England was established towards the end of the 17th century, and London was now handling 80% of England's imports and almost 70% of its exports. It should be noted that London was never a place where goods were manufactured, but a place where goods were traded.

Politics, The Industrial Revolution & London's Railway Age

In 1707, the Kingdom of Great Britain came to be as the English and Scottish parliaments came together with the Acts of Union. London at the time was expanding in every direction: in the west towards Mayfair, the east saw an expansion of the Port of London, and bridges across the river allowed London to grow towards the south.

A new phenomenon in London at the time was the coffeehouse where newspapers could be read, as printing presses became common. Fleet Street became synonymous with news.

Eighteenth century London was also rife with crime with the death penalty being using for the vast majority of crimes. Public hangings, in areas such as Marble Arch, were common and big public spectacles.

London went through a radical change in the 1800s. It became the world's largest city and during the 19th century its population exploded from 1 million to 6.7 million.

Also during the 19th century, the invention of the steam train and its railways, under Queen Victoria's reign transformed London, but the building of new railways meant the demolition of many buildings. Most areas affected by the demolition were poor areas due to the easy approval by government authorities.

London's maiden railway line was commissioned in February 1836 between Deptford and Bermondsey. The 1840s, experienced railway boom, which also saw the arrival of long distance railway travel. The introduction of the railways saw a massive rise in population and London's area became larger than ever before.

Mere years later, in 1863, London unveiled the world's first underground railway running from Paddington to Farringdon.

Meanwhile, in 1855, Joseph Bazalgette led a team of workers who constructed over 2,000km of tunnels in London's first sewage system. The death rate in London dropped dramatically as living conditions improved.

London's population began to become more international, as Irish settlers moved over during the Great Famine in the mid-1850s. People from poorer parts of Europe emigrated to London, as did many from colonial countries.

World Wars and the 20th Century London

London suffered heavily during World War I but was still the capital of a massive empire. Between World War I and II, London continued to expand geographically as the transport system expanded and allowed people to live in the suburbs; car ownership also facilitated this.

London's unemployment grew rapidly during the Great Depression of the 1930s, only to be followed by World War II. During The Blitz, London suffered extensive damage, and again fires raged through the City of London destroying it. Over one million houses in London were destroyed, and the death toll reached 40,000. Many escaped to the countryside, fearing for their lives.

London went through a massive rebuilding project after WWII, and the 1950s and 1960s saw big tower blocks being built to house Londoners. During this time, many immigrants came to the city from the Commonwealth countries – Indians, Jamaicans, Pakistanis and Bangladeshis made their way to the city, making it a truly multicultural place to live.

London's population was decreasing, though, and had dropped from 8.6 million before WWII to 6.8 million in the 1980s. This began to increase again from the mid-1980s onwards.

Present Day London

London today is a cosmopolitan city with international repute. The city has an official population of more than 8.6 million people, matching its peak in 1939. The city is still growing, however, and its population is expected to reach 10 million by 2029.

London has twenty post codes, thirty-two boroughs and, at the time of writing, has Boris Johnson as its mayor.

The city has not lost its unique historical influence, though, as it boasts four heritage sites: Kew Gardens; the areas of the Palace of Westminster, St Margaret's Church and Westminster Abbey; the Tower of London; and Maritime Greenwich.

London has also transformed into an education hub with thousands of students from around the world flocking to the city annually in search of fine education. The city boasts high caliber colleges like the London school of Economics, Royal Academy of Music and the London Business School.

In terms of tourism, London attracts over fourteen million tourists annually and possesses a vibrant economy. Measured in terms of international visitors, London is the most visited city in the world.

Today's London is truly amazing. It has evolved to become the multicultural center of Europe and an economic, educational and tourist hub. The future of the city looks brighter than ever.

London Today: An Overview

London is a fascinating city: it is a place where people from all walks of life and cultures live together; it is a global economic powerhouse with the City of London's Stock Exchange and Canary Wharf; and it is a historic city that still thrives to this day, where brand new glass flats and offices surround a 950-year-old castle. London is the largest city in Western Europe and it is a place that once you have visited once, you will almost certainly want to come back for more.

Throughout your trip, you will find a variety of world class attractions, from art galleries to monuments, and theatres, restaurants and more. No matter what time of year you visit, you will find something different and unique going on in the city.

The People of London – Demographics

Despite what the media may have you think, London's cultural background is very diverse. Only 45% of people in London are of a white British origin, 15% are other white, 18% are Asian, 13% are black, 5% are mixed and 4% classify themselves as 'other'. As you can see, the city is incredibly diverse.

In terms of wealth, London is a city of two extremes. Travelling through central London areas such as Mayfair and Kensington, it is not uncommon to walk past homes worth £30 million or more. Venture outside of the areas of the wealthy and you will discover how 27% of Londoners are officially classified as living in poverty.

Local customs and etiquette
Attitudes

Londoners personas are commonly described as being 'straight faced'; they do not walk around with giant smiles on their faces, nor do they get involved in anything that doesn't directly concern them: watching a film in a cinema will not illicit cheers or weeping, nor does anyone care how others dress.

Having said this, many perceive this indifference as being rude. This is not the case: Londoners *are* friendly and sociable people. It's just that most Londoners work such long hours (and have such long commutes) that they aren't always smiling. If you ask a Londoner for the time, or directions, you will likely encounter a warm smile and they'll politely help you. It's breaking that first barrier that can be the problem for Londoners.

Topics of conversation
Londoners are generally less chatty than other Brits, and the general attitude around the city is "I'll live my life, you live yours".

As far as conversations go - Londoners, and Brits in general – are *very* good at small talk. Chats about the weather, the news, travel and many other subjects are common.

However, you should know that some subjects are best avoided: money, sex, politics and age, for example. Racism and offensive jokes are not tolerated, nor are criticisms of our culture. These topics are likely to be met with a cold stare.

Tipping
Tipping practices vary wildly across the world, and in London there are a certain set of rules to abide by. You should follow the UK tipping practices and not those of your home country.

Every person in employment in the UK earns at least the minimum wage. As of early 2016, this is £6.70 an hour for those aged 21 and over, and £7.20 for those aged at least 25. For those aged 18 to 20, it is £5.30 an hour. This is on par with many other major nations. Every employer is required to pay their employees the minimum wage or higher, and tips cannot be used to make up the minimum wage.

However, in order to have a "normal standard of living", there is also a "living wage". This is a non-compulsory advisory for employers who wish to ensure their employees can afford to live in the city. Employers may choose the pay this on a voluntary basis. The London Living Wage is currently £9.40 an hour.

Most people you will come into contact with in customer-focused roles do not earn the £9.40 living wage and likely earn the minimum wage – there is a £2.20 to £2.70 per hour gap between these two wage levels. Therefore, many people rely on tips in order to make up the rest of their income. The cost of living in London is extremely high, and therefore tips make a major difference to many people.

Tips are NOT compulsory in the UK on any service. If a service charge has been added to your bill, you can request that it be removed and the service provider *must* oblige. However, due to the fact that most employees in customer-service roles earn so little, tips are very much appreciated.

In the UK the most common form of tip is at a restaurant. Here a 10% to 15% tip on the final price of the bill is the norm. If a restaurant has added on a "service charge", that is the equivalent of the tip. You can choose to remove it if you do not feel the service was adequate. It is bad form to not tip if you received a good level of service, but tips are – of course – optional. In London, people do not tip at fast food locations or for take-away meals. Tips in bars and pubs are also not commonplace.

Taxi services merit the second most common form of tip. Here 10% is more than enough; most people will round up to the nearest £1 or £5 depending on the journey length to avoid the taxi driver having to dig for change.

In the hospitality industry, the American form of tipping is slowly making its way across to the UK. It is not very common to tip for help from a concierge service or for help with luggage at a hotel, but if the service was exceptional, a small tip is highly appreciated – £1 to £3 is more than enough. This is still a relatively rare occurrence but is becoming more commonplace.

Finally, if you are on an excursion, walking tour, bus tour or private guided tour, tips are now becoming commonplace for these. This is particularly the case for longer guided tours lasting several hours. A tip of £3 to £5 is a nice gesture for an enjoyable tour, and anything more than that would be seen as very generous.

Public transport

If you're using our public transport system and are on the "metro", "subway" or "underground", Londoner's call this it the *tube* - pronounced 'chewb' (not 'toob'). The tube has several rules, laws and regulations. For example, it is a legal requirement to let people off the train before boarding; this means standing to one side of the doors.

Once on the train, if you manage to get hold of a seat, you should give up your seat to any disabled, elderly or pregnant passengers – once again, this is a legal requirement. Trains are only at stations for a few seconds and it is therefore customary to be ready to leave the train *before* it stops at a station.

Tube etiquette dictates that you do not make eye contact. Do not stare at the person in front of you or anyone else on the carriage. Would you feel comfortable with someone staring at you on your 40-minute journey into work? We wouldn't. Instead, *Transport for London*, has devised the clever placing of adverts just above the seats so you can glance up and read that advert for *Wellmen* dozens of times on your trip. Better still, close your eyes and plug in your earphones, or bring a book.

Shopping

When handling money in a shop, it is customary to be polite. As you pay you say 'thanks', again when you get your receipt or change, and then one final time as you leave. Yes, we are that polite.

When asking for something the correct phrase is "May I have.." or "Could I have" but never "I need…" or "I want…".

Accents

If you ever meet a true East Londoner, or a Cockney as they are known, you may have a bit of trouble understanding them. The accent is unique and sometimes they may even use (the now dying) Cockney rhyming slang. Essentially these are words and expression which rhyme with real English words. For example, if some tells you to 'take the *apples and pears*', that means 'take the stairs'.

Cockney Rhyming Slang is something that you will never hear in a professional context, and it is extremely unlikely you will encounter it at all, but if you do, you will now have some idea of what's going on.

Many people in London have an accent known as received pronunciation (RP), also known as the Queen's English or BBC English. However, as Londoners are made up from people from all around the world, you will likely encounter a wide variety of accents throughout your stay.

Americanisms

Americanisms (American versions of British words) are pet peeves of Londoners. If you're asking for the restroom, a corndog, an elevator, the subway, where the start of the 'line' is, asking for 'the check', or using any other non-British English word or phrase, this can be a problem.

In the hospitality trade, most employees are aware and used to hearing American English. In other places you may well be asked what these words mean: either because the people doesn't know, or because they want to pretend they don't.

Learning a few of our English words and phrases can make a big difference to your visit to London. Below is our guide to some of the common British phrases you may hear or use.

Useful phrases

British English	International English
Tube (pronounced "chewb")	Metro, subway or Underground
Toilet	Bathroom or Restroom
Chips	Fries (thick)
Crisps	Chips (like Lays, McCoys, Walkers)
Ground Floor	First Floor
First Floor	Second Floor (and so on)
Biscuit	Cookie
Sweets	Candy
Note	Bill
Bill	Check
Queue	Line
Jumper/Hoodie	Sweater
Mobile Phone	Cell Phone

Weather

London is a city that experiences the full force of the four seasons, so the timing of your visit will have a large impact on the clothes you bring, as well as some of the activities you may wish to do.
The coldest month is usually February. The average low is about 2 °C (35 °F), but there will be occasional drops below freezing throughout both January and February. Snowfall varies: some years there is none at all; other years, London's transport system comes to a halt despite only a few inches of the white stuff.

Summer temperatures are not quite as warm as some may expect, with average highs lying around 22 °C (72 °F), though the city environment makes it feel much warmer. Even at these temperatures the non-air conditioned underground lines are swelteringly hot. Some days in the summer may reach closer to 30 °C (85 °F), and summer 2015's heatwave even saw highs topping 36 °C (97°F). In the evenings, temperatures tend to cool down quickly and we recommend carrying a light jumper or hoodie with you.

Spring and Autumn feel like they take up the majority of the year. From March to June, and September to November, expect highs of between 10°C and 20°C, and lows between 4°C and 11°C.

Rainfall is relatively consistent throughout the year, with monthly rainfall averaging between 46mm (1.7 inches) and 77mm (3 inches). Each month has 9 to 12 rainy days on average, with Autumn being the wettest season. February is the month that experiences the least rain, but even this is only a marginal difference; averages say that October is generally the wettest month.

Month by Month Temperature Averages:
Temperatures are averages, the first is in Celsius, followed by Fahrenheit.

	Low (C/F)	High (C/F)
January	2/35	7/44
February	2/35	7/44
March	4/39	11/52
April	5/41	13/55
May	8/46	17/63
June	11/51	20/68
July	13/55	22/72
August	13/55	22/72
September	11/51	19/66
October	8/46	15/59
November	5/41	10/50
December	3/37	7/44

More important considerations
Currency
In London, the Pound Sterling is used as the form of currency. No other forms of currency is accepted as a legal form of payment. Although, the UK is part of the European Union, where many countries use the Euro (€), the UK has not adopted it as its currency.

One pound is written as £1. This is sub-divided into 100 pennies, 'p' or pence – these terms are used interchangeably. Coins available in the UK are 1p, 2p, 5p, 10p, 20p, 50p, £1, £2 and the very rare (and actually collectable) £5.

Paper based currency are called 'notes', and not 'bills' as they are called in the US. These are available in denominations of £5, £10, £20 and £50. It should be noted that £50 notes are sometimes not accepted by smaller stores due to their high value and fear of forgery, so be aware of this when exchanging your cash for pounds. Sometimes a manager may need to be called for £50 notes to be verified before they are accepted, even at larger stores. All coins and notes bare the head of Queen Elizabeth II on them.

Fun Tip: New coin designs are regularly issued, so be sure to check out what is on the back of your coins. The most elaborate designs are on the large £2 coins – these vary greatly; you may come across a design of St. Paul's Cathedral, another of the Magna Carta, and even a commemoration of the first world war, amongst dozens of others. Smaller denominations of coins also feature unique designs.

Making Phone Calls

Make sure your mobile phone will work in the UK before visiting. Modern smartphones will most likely work everywhere. However, some older models, and non-smartphones, may be limited to your home country or region. Be sure to check before travelling.

You should also be aware of roaming charges when visiting the UK. Calls and text messages will often cost significantly more than they do back home. You may also be charged to receive calls and messages too. Data, in particular, can be extremely expensive so be sure to check with your network provider whether they offer any roaming deals or packages.

Once in the UK, you will need to dial an international code to make calls. For calls to the UK, you should add 0044 or +44 before the phone number you are calling. Phone numbers in the UK generally begin with 01 if outside London, and 02 within London.
So, if you are dialling a central London number from your cell phone, you would call 0044(0)207 or +44(0)207, then the rest of the number. The zero in brackets is not dialled from international phones.

If you need to make international phone calls, depending on how your network provider has set this up, you may need to enter your country's international dialling code, followed by the phone number. For the USA, for example, you would need to add +1 (or 001) before the phone number.

Internet Access:

London has excellent mobile phone signal for both data and calls across all networks. However, data access when roaming with your home mobile phone will often be very expensive for international visitors, so you are best sticking to Wi-Fi hotspots when you need data.

Most hotels include unlimited free Wi-Fi in the cost of your room. When out and about, many restaurants also provide this for their diners. McDonalds's and Starbucks provide free Wi-Fi access around town at their locations. If you happen to walk past an Apple Store, you can use their Wi-Fi too. Many coffee shops and restaurants also provide free Wi-Fi, although you may have to register or a code for access.

The City of London area is covered with free street-wide Wi-Fi almost everywhere too. Virgin Media provides free Wi-Fi on the tube at stations and platforms for some UK mobile phone users; there are also paid access passes available. Many public libraries and museums also provide free access.

Important: Remember that you will need plug adapters that work in the UK. These are NOT the same as in the rest of Europe. The UK uses a three-pronged design, as opposed to continental Europe's two prongs.

Also, be sure to check the voltage of your devices before bringing them over. The UK runs on 230-240V unlike some region's 100V (e.g. the US), so you will need a power inverter for some items. If you plug the 100V items in directly with an adapter but without an inverter, they will likely burn or blow.

Many items are now able to be connected without an inverter, and simply require an adapter. Check the power brick of your appliance and make sure it supports either 230V or 240V. Continental European items usually run on 230V, so only an adapter is required for these.

Getting to London

Before you begin to explore the city, you must first get here. This section covers all your options on how to reach England's capital.

Flying

As the UK is a fairly isolated island, most visitors who arrive in London do so by plane. The airports in London when combined make up the largest city airport system in the world, carrying the highest number of passengers. When flying into London, there are five main airports to consider. These are listed in size, with the largest first:

London Heathrow Airport

Heathrow is the busiest airport in Europe in terms of passenger traffic and the most popular of London's airports. It is located 22km from central London, or 12 miles. It has five terminals, of which four are operational. Terminal 1 is currently closed and will be demolished. The airport's plan is to gradually reduce the number of terminals but to make each one larger, thereby easing passenger transfers. The airport has two runways.

Public transport

Heathrow is well linked with public transport. The transfer option that works best for you may well depend on where you will be staying whilst in London:

Underground – The Piccadilly line on the London underground goes all the way to Heathrow with three stops for passengers - Terminals 2 and 3; Terminal 4 and Terminal 5. Passengers should leave at the most appropriate stop as transferring between terminals can be time-consuming. Journey times are about 40 to 50 minutes from central London.

The cash fare between central London and Heathrow is £6 per person. The oyster fare is £3.10 off-peak, and £5.10 during peak hours. This is the most affordable rail option.

Heathrow Express – This is a non-stop National Rail train service that takes 15 minutes from Heathrow Central (Terminals 2 and 3) to London Paddington Station. Trains depart every 15 minutes. The journey time for trains to and from Terminal 5 is 21 minutes. Those arriving and departing from Terminal 4 can make use of the free Terminal 4 shuttle service to and from Heathrow Central and Terminal 4 – this shuttle takes 4 minutes. A walk-up adult fare is £26 one-way or £40 return for standard class. Children 15 and under travel free with a fare-paying adult. Tickets booked in advance can be as low as £6.99 one-way and £11.90 return depending on how far in advance you book. If you are staying in the Paddington area, want a speedy transfer, and can book in advance, the Express service offers fantastic value for money.

Heathrow Connect – This is a National Rail service that takes 27 minutes from Heathrow Central to London Paddington station. It follows the same route as the Heathrow Express, but stops along the way at up to five other stations. Trains leave every 30 minutes. The train does not serve Terminal 4 or 5, but only Heathrow Central (Terminals 2 and 3). A free shuttle train is available to Terminal 4.

Passengers wishing to travel to terminal 5 will need to take free bus transportation from within the terminal itself (not the rail station). As such, if you are travelling to Terminal 5, we do not recommend this option. The Express service or Underground service is easier and will most likely be faster too. It may also be cheaper. One-way tickets between Heathrow and Paddington cost £10.10 one-way, or £20.20 return.

South West Trains – From Heathrow Central Bus Station you can catch a red London bus (number 285) to Feltham railway station (a fare is payable). From there, you can catch a National Rail train to London Waterloo Station; there are trains every 10 minutes. Trains also run to Twickenham, Richmond, Clapham Junction, Vauxhall, Putney and Hounslow – these all run at 30 minute intervals (less frequently on Sundays). Journeys to/from the airport are 30 to 45 minutes. An anytime fare is £6.90 each way. To be honest, due to the transfer time involved and the need to get a bus, we would recommend you use the Underground if travelling between Waterloo and Heathrow, changing at Green Park Station.

Bus/Coach – All these services arrive and depart from Heathrow Central Bus station for Terminals 2 and 3. Some also operate from bus stations at Terminals 4 and 5. Otherwise a free transfer will be needed. National Express and Oxford Bus Company both operate services between Heathrow and London Victoria Coach station. Green Line route 724 goes to St. Alban's. The journey time is 45 to 60 minutes in normal conditions, and up to 2 hours in traffic. Coach prices are £6 to £8 when booked in advance.

If traveling between midnight and 5:00am, the night-bus route N9 operates, taking you to various locations in central London including Hammersmith, Trafalgar Square and terminating in Aldgate. The N9 price is £1.50 on an Oyster or contactless payment card (more on Oyster cards later in the travel chapter). London buses do not take cash.

Other transport

Car – Driving into central London is not recommended. Public transport is good around the city, parking is expensive and you will have to pay a daily fee, called the 'Congestion Charge', of £11.50 per day if entering central London (more on this in the travel section).

If you still insist on driving, follow directions to the Heathrow area exit tunnel and then follow the M4 motorway which will take you to central London. Make sure you have a map or GPS device as London is complicated enough to navigate for locals, let alone visitors! The journey will take 45 to 60 minutes to central London if you do not encounter traffic. This journey time can double in rush hour traffic.

Taxi – A ride in a black taxi (cab) to central London will vary depending on where you want to go specifically, but the journey will typically take 30 to 60 minutes, provided there is no traffic. The fare will be anywhere from £45 to £85 typically. There are no extra charges for luggage or additional passengers but a £2.80 charge applies for taxi journeys starting at Heathrow. Note that not all taxis accept debit or credit cards and there is an extra charge of up to 10% of the fare for paying by card. No charge will apply from October 2016.

Minicabs – You can also get private hire minicabs. These must be booked in advance; it is illegal to take one that has not been booked in advance. Drivers will usually meet you at the flight arrivals area in the terminal. Heathrow Airport officially recommends **www.greentomatocars.com** if booking a minicab. They use environmentally-friendly hybrid cars. Book online or call +44(0)208 568 0022 for a quote. Calling may give you a lower quote.

Uber – This is also another popular option, allowing you to book a cab from your smartphone on demand. There are several categories of car you can book ranging from an UberPool where you share a ride with others going the same way, to a standard car, or a luxury vehicle. You will get an estimated price before you confirm your vehicle – estimates range from £29 to £94 one-way. Get $20/£10 free credit by using our exclusive sign-up link at **http://uber.com/invite/uberindependentguides** or enter "uberindependentguides" as a voucher code when using the app for the first time.

Taxis, Ubers and Minicabs can be especially good value when you are travelling in a group. Instead of using public transport and each paying an individual fare, you can all ride for one fee.

London Gatwick Airport

Gatwick is London's second largest airport and is located 29.5miles (47.5km) from central London, about twice as far out at Heathrow. It has two terminals - North and South - and one runway which is the world's busiest "single-use runway". Many charter airlines operate from Gatwick, as well as scheduled airlines. The two terminals are connected by an automated people-mover.

Public transport

Rail – There are no Underground services to this airport. National Rail services operate to and from London Victoria and London Bridge stations and the "Gatwick Airport" rail station.

The **Gatwick Express** service is a non-stop train journey taking about 30 minutes between central London and the airport; there are trains every 15 minutes on this route. Standard Class tickets are £19.90 each way for adults, £34.90 return, or £9.95 each way for children, £17.45 return. First Class tickets are £29.00 for adults and £14.50 for children each way, or £56.00 and £28.00 respectively for a return ticket.

A discount of 10% is available for tickets that are pre-booked online. You can also use contactless payment cards and Oyster cards on this route to avoid having to purchase a physical ticket in advance. These fares are the same price as the on-the-day fare. Pre-booked tickets may therefore be cheaper in this case.

Southern Railways and Thameslink also provide services between Gatwick and central London. These trains make more stops than the Gatwick Express but are also substantially cheaper. There also a wider variety of starting points for your journey: London Victoria, London Bridge, London Charing Cross, London Waterloo East, City Thameslink, London Blackfriars, London Kings Cross and London Liverpool Street. Journey times vary between 30 and 53 minutes.

Single adult fares vary depending on which station you are travelling from, and at what time. These range between £9.40 and £15.40 for a one-way single ticket in standard class for adults. Single child fares vary between £4.70 and £9.95.

We recommend this option over the Gatwick Express as the time difference for a lot of the trains is negligible and the savings can be substantial – especially for a group. Purchase the "Anytime" tickets online or at the station – the "advance" tickets only allow you to travel on a certain train which could easily be missed due to the flight, immigration or baggage delays.

Coach/Bus – National Express coach tickets from Victoria Coach Station to Gatwick airport cost £8 on average each way, with a journey time of 1 hour 5 minutes to 1 hour 25 minutes. EasyBus tickets (note you do not have to be an EasyJet customer to use this service) start at £2 each way if booked far in advance from Earl's Court to Gatwick with a journey time of approximately 1 hour 5 minutes. Terravision is another operator with fares starting at £6.

Other transport

Car – From wherever you are in London, head south of the city until you reach the M25 London Orbital, at junction 7 of the M25 head south-bound on the M23. Exit/junction number 9 is for Gatwick Airport. Follow the local signs from there. We do not recommend you drive to and from your London accommodation due to the long journey time and expense; a train is usually a much better option for most people.

Taxi – Gatwick says the only official service is "Airport Cars Gatwick" and it is possible to book these online at **http://taxis.gatwickairport.com/bookings/taxi.html**. We do not recommend you take a taxi to and from your hotel due to the long journey time and expense, a train will usually be a better option. A pre-booked private minicab will cost £45 to £60 each way depending on the company. A local black taxi will cost in excess of £100 each way.

Uber – This is also another popular option, allowing you to book a cab from your smartphone on demand. There are several categories of car you can book depending on your needs. You will get an estimated price before you confirm your vehicle. Fares generally run between £79 and £130 one-way depending on location. Get $20/£10 free credit by using our exclusive sign-up link at **http://uber.com/invite/uberindependentguides** or enter "uberindependentguides" as a voucher code when using the app for the first time.

London Stansted Airport

Stansted Airport lies 30 miles, or 48 kilometres, north-east of central London. It is the newest large passenger airport in London. Stansted is a breeze to get through with a beautiful glass terminal meaning lots of natural light fills the space, making it feel spacious. It is not as busy as Gatwick and Heathrow airports, and therefore makes for a more pleasant experience.

This airport is mainly targeted at European travelers, though a few flights to long-haul destinations have been added in recent years. It is, however, still a major airport with over 19 million passengers a year traveling through it.

Public Transport

Stansted Express Train – Departs every 15 minutes with a journey time of 47 minutes each way from London Liverpool Street. You can also get the Stansted Express from Stratford (with a change at Tottenham Hale) or directly from Tottenham Hale station itself.

On the day tickets are £18 to £19 each way (depending on your start point), or £30 to £32 return for adults. First class fares are approximately £10 more expensive each way and include a FastTrack airport security pass. Pre-booked tickets start at £7.50 each way – you must specify a travel date, but not time. Group offers are also available for parties of 3 or 4 passengers.

Coach – National Express coach tickets start at £6 per person each way with journey times of 1 hour 30 minutes to 1 hour 45 minutes. EasyBus tickets start at £2 per person each way with journey times of approximately 1 hour 15 minutes to 1 hour 30 minutes. Terravision also provides coach services with similar prices to National Express. Pick up points are available in central and East London.

Other transport
Car – Join the M11 at Junction 8, follow the M11 until you reach the North Circular road (A406). You are now in East London. Please have a navigation device with you for the rest of the journey as it very much depends on where you would like to go in London itself. We do not recommend driving for most people as it is a long drive (over an hour) and can be done far more quickly by train.

Taxi and Uber – We do not recommend you take a taxi to and from your hotel due to the long journey time and expense. A train will usually be a much better option. In a cab, the journey will take 70 to 80 minutes and will cost about £95 to £110. There is no taxi rank at the airport; these must be pre-booked in advance with London Black Cabs. This can be done at arrivals. A mini cab may be cheaper.

An Uber between the airport and central London is priced at between £58 and £119 depending on the size of car you request, and where you are travelling to. Get $20/£10 free credit by using our exclusive sign-up link at **http://uber.com/invite/uberindependentguides** or enter "uberindependentguides" as a voucher code when using the app for the first time.

London Luton
London Luton is another of London's many airports and it consists mainly of low-cost carriers from across Europe. There are some charter routes out of the airport to North Africa and Asia but these are few and far between. Luton is located 35 miles or 56.5km north of central London.

One of the big advantages with Luton is its size – because it is still relatively small, you can get through the airport quite quickly. It still, however, sees over 10.5 million passengers come through its doors every year and is growing rapidly.

Public Transport
Rail – Journeys from central London to "Luton Airport Parkway" station are operated by Thameslink and East Midland Trains. Trains are available from London Blackfairs and London St. Pancras stations. Journey times vary considerably – there is one fast train per hour from St. Pancras where the journey time is a mere 20 minutes. Other journeys vary from 39 to 55 minutes.

Luton has an unusual situation where the rail station is not directly located in the airport itself; instead it is 1 mile west of the airport, and both are linked by a shuttle bus that runs every 10 minutes during the day. The shuttle bus journey takes an additional 10 minutes.

Coach – Terravision, National Express and EasyBus all provide shuttle services from central London directly to London Luton airport. Transfer time is 50 to 80 minutes depending on where you board. Prices are generally between £8 and £12 each way. Promotional fares from £2 are sometimes available, if booked well in advance.

Other Transport
Car – This is a fairly easy car journey with a typical journey time of 45 minutes to 1 hour 15 minutes depending on the traffic you encounter. From Luton Airport you will need to follow signs for the M1 motorway going south, when in the suburbs of London, you will briefly join the A406 (North Circular Road). Then exit onto the A41 (Hendon Way), and finally follow Finchley Road to reach central London. From here, we recommend you use a GPS device to reach your destination.

Taxi and Uber – You can get a black London cab directly from the taxi rank outside the main terminal. You can also make a reservation with one of the many mini-cabs firms that operate.

With an Uber, expect to pay between £50 and £129 for the journey depending on what type of car you get and the destination. Get $20/£10 free credit by using our exclusive sign-up link at **http://uber.com/invite/uberindependentguides** or enter "uberindependentguides" as a voucher code when using the app for the first time.

London City Airport
This is the most centrally located of all the airports, being only 6 miles from central London, making it a breeze to get to. It is rather small and caters mostly for business travelers. Its destinations are mostly short haul in Europe, as well as New York. This airport also has great connections across the UK. Just 3.6 million passengers use the airport yearly, and it is the least busy of London's airports.

Due to the short runway length and its location, the airplanes used here are all relatively small – the largest takes just 132 passengers.

Public Transport
DLR – Transport for London operates the DLR service, which is integrated with the Underground system. Bank Station to London City Airport is only 22 minutes on the DLR with fantastic views of East London along the way. Oyster Card and contactless card fares are £3.30 during peak times, and £2.80 off-peak. The cash fare is £4.90.

Other transport
Driving – We do not recommend driving to London City Airport and around London in general. Avis, Budget, Europcar and Hertz operate rental locations at the airport. The driving time will take between 35 minutes and 1 hour depending on where you are going to in central London.

Taxi and **Uber** – Taxi prices are metered from London City Airport to central London. Expect to pay about £35 each way between the airport and Covent Garden, £40 to Piccadilly and £50 to Bayswater. Uber prices average £20 to £30 from most places in central London.

Rail to London
National Rail
If you are travelling from across the UK to London, you will arrive in one of the main London terminals. These are: **Paddington** (trains to and from Oxford, Bristol, South Wales, Bath, Exeter, Plymouth), **Marylebone** (Warwick, plus all Euston's destinations), **Euston** (Birmingham, North Wales, Liverpool, Manchester, Glasgow and Scotland), **St. Pancras** (Leicester, Nottingham, Sheffield, Leeds and Dover), **Kings Cross** (Leeds, York, Newcastle, Edinburgh and Scotland), **Liverpool Street** (Norwich and Cambridge), **Charing Cross** (Dover), **Waterloo** (Brighton, Portsmouth, Southampton, Exeter) and **Victoria** (Brighton and Dover).

All these stations are located in Zone 1 in central London. Wherever you arrive in central London, chances are your next stop will be either the tube or a taxi to get to your final destination.

International Rail – Eurostar and Eurotunnel:

London is connected to continental Europe via a 50km underwater rail link (known as the Channel Tunnel – or 'Chunnel' for short) that connects Folkestone in south-east England with Calais in the north of France. The journey time from one side to the other is about 35 minutes.

There are two main passenger rail services that operate through the Chunnel – the Eurostar and Eurotunnel services.

Eurostar

The Eurostar is a high-speed passenger train like many others used throughout Europe – France's TGV is probably the most famous. As the train crosses international borders and the UK is not part of the Schengen agreement, there are a few extra security procedures to be aware of that do not apply to most other trains.

You will need to check-in for your Eurostar train at least 30 minutes before departure. This is simply a case of scanning your ticket at the automated barriers. Then you will go through airport-style security (although here you can bring liquids with you) with a metal detector and an X-Ray baggage scan. Then you will go through passport control and enter the departure lounge. You will then board your train when it is announced. On Eurostar services, you take all luggage with you and must be able to physically carry this onto the train.

When you reach the other end, you simply step off the train. When arriving into the UK you may be selected for additional customs checks.

Travel times and 'starting from' prices:
London to Calais – 1 hour 5 minutes, £65
London to Lille – 1 hour 20 minutes, £65
London to Brussels – 1 hour 51 minutes, £69
London to Paris – 2 hours 15 minutes, £72
London to Disneyland Paris – 2 hour 35 minutes, £69

Journey times stated above are for the fastest trains. Slower trains may add a few minutes onto your travel time. The prices are 'starting at' return prices for one adult. Child and youth fares are also available, which will save you a few pounds each way.

Prices increase when a pre-set allocation of cheaper seats has sold out. Occasional sales are also available during slower periods of the year; prices are typically £10 cheaper during these sales.

There are also 'direct' services from London to the south of France – destinations include Lyon, Avignon and Marseille, as well as a seasonal ski service.

Eurostar has also announced that they will begin a direct service between London and Amsterdam in December 2016.

If you are travelling into London from continental Europe, most countries are linked by high-speed rail. It is often easy enough to reach Paris and then hop on a Eurostar to London.

Eurotunnel
The Eurotunnel is another service that uses the Chunnel, linking Folkestone and Calais. This service allows you take your vehicle across from the UK to continental Europe and vice versa. This means you can drive a lorry, car, motorhome or motorbike onto the Eurotunnel train which then travels through the Channel Tunnel. The crossing time is just 35 minutes and, if driving between the continent and the UK, it is a fantastic and fast way to get across.

Prices vary on the length of trip – a one-day or overnight trip begins at £23 each way; a 5-day trip starts at £59; other trips start at £76 each way. This can work out to be a very affordable price per passenger. Prices are per vehicle and include all passengers inside it.

The Eurotunnel terminal at Folkestone is a 75-mile drive from central London (about 1 hour 45 minutes to 2 hours' driving time). The route is via the M20 until reaching the M25 (London's Orbital Motorway). A GPS Navigation device is strongly recommended for this journey.

Ferry Services

Ferry services are available into ports around the UK, with several locations a short drive from London. These ferries carry your vehicle, as well as passengers, between the UK and the rest of Europe. Many coach companies also use the Ferry services to access the UK on excursions between London and Continental Europe.

Calais (France) to Dover (England) is the shortest ferry trip at just 90 minutes. Dunkirk (France) to Dover is another option – this trip is about 2 hours.

Ferries between France and Spain, arriving into the UK ports of Portsmouth, Poole and Plymouth are also available. These are longer journeys ranging from 6 hours to an overnight trip with a sleeping cabin onboard.

Finally, ferry crossings from Rotterdam (The Netherlands) and Esbjerg (Denmark) are also available. Rotterdam is a 6-hour crossing, and Esbjerg is an 18-hour crossing.

Transport in London

Transport has always been, and will always be, fundamental to London. The city is large and getting 8.6 million residents around, plus millions of visitors every year, is an incredible feat.

London has always innovated in this respect, constructing the world's first underground railway in the 1860s. It has one of the largest bus fleets in the world with over 9,000 buses on 675 routes. That is, of course, in addition to the Docklands Light Railway, National Rail services, the London Overground, the river services, trams and taxis, which are all integral to London's transport needs.

London's public transport system is incredibly varied and this section goes into a lot of detail. If you will be spending all your time in central London only (and using public transport), then the Oyster Card, Bus and Underground sections will be the most relevant to you. If you are planning on venturing further afield, there is a huge amount of other important information covered here.

Driving

Roads in London can be cumbersome to drive on. Many roads are in a bad state and drivers from many other cities may be surprised at how narrow some of them are. There is no simple road system either – London has expanded from a series of villages to a huge city with no grid-based system like New York; therefore, a GPS navigation system and/or a map is highly recommended.

Visitors must also be aware of driving laws in the UK, which may differ from others around the world:

* Drivers and all passengers must always expected to fasten their seatbelts.
* Restraints or car seats are mandatory for children.
* Drivers should not stop near pedestrian crossings – a zone is marked with zig-zag lines before and after the crossing where it is forbidden to stop.
* Stay out of bus lanes during the hours displayed on road signs.
* Certain vehicles and people many not drive on motorways; this includes provisional driving license holders, motorcycles under 50cc, cyclists and more. Pedestrians and horse riders are also not permitted.
* You may only overtake another vehicle on the right-hand side of it. You should always drive in the left-hand lane, unless overtaking, if the road is clear.

* Do not exceed the speed limits which are clearly marked on all roads, with regular reminders.
* You must not drive whilst on your mobile phone – this is illegal. Driving while distracted, and not in proper control of your vehicle, is a prosecutable offence.
* Some roads are 'Red Routes' which means that there must be no stopping at any time. These are clearly signposted.
* Drivers must stop for pedestrians at crossings – whether they are already crossing, whether they are approaching a crossing, or whether they are already waiting to cross. The pedestrian must finish crossing completely before the driver continues.
* You cannot turn left or right when a traffic light is red under any circumstances, unless there is a specific arrow for your direction that is lit up in green.
* Motorcyclists must wear helmets at all times while riding.
* Box junctions are yellow crisscrossed boxes drawn onto the ground at some crossings. It is illegal to stop in this box, so do not enter at unless your exit is clear.
* Parking can be tricky. If a road has a single yellow line, parking is allowed at certain times of day – a sign will indicate this. Double yellow lines mean no parking at any time. Red lines mean no stopping at any time, even to let passengers in and out, in addition to no parking.

These are merely a few of the country's driving laws. If you are planning on driving, we advise you fully research this in advance.

The Congestion Charge
Driving a car is heavily discouraged in London, particularly in the city centre. In 2003, Ken Livingstone, then Mayor of London, implemented a traffic reduction method called the Congestion Charge (CC) – this is a toll on drivers who come into the centre of London by road. The aim was to reduce the congestion in London, removing cars and lorries from the road. The money from this charge funds improvements to the road and public transport system.

As of May 2016, the charge is £11.50 per day between the hours of 9:00am and 6:00pm, Monday to Friday. The Congestion Charge area applies to much of central London, and almost all the main attractions in London are within the charging area. Before reaching an area that is subject to the Congestion Charge, road signs will warn you and indicate how to avoid it well in advance.

You have until midnight to pay the day rate of the CC; you can also pay the next day, when the charge increases to £14. If you fail to pay the charge, you will be fined. If you are in a rental car, the exact same thing applies – fail to pay the charge, and you will be fined (£65 to £130). This can be very costly over a long stay.

Filling Up
The place where you get your fuel from – usual petrol or diesel is called a "petrol station" in the UK. For the Americans, this is where you fill up your car with 'gas' – in the UK this is called either 'petrol' or 'diesel' – be sure to know which one your car takes. Petrol stations are few and far between in central London and therefore queues can be long at each one. Major petrol stations in central London include:
* Esso – 115 Maida Vale, London, W9 1UP. Open 24/7.
* Esso – 393 Edgware Road, London, W2 1BT. Open 24/7.
* Esso – 77 Park Lane, London, W1K 7HB
* Shell – 106 Old Brompton Road, London, SW7 3RA
* BP – 238 Kennington Lane, London, SE11 5RD. Open 24/7
* Texaco – 212 Kennington Road, London, SE11 6PR

Parking
As well as the cost of the car rental, insurance, fuel, and the Congestion Charge, there is the cost of parking.

Parking in central London can be challenging, so locating car parks closest to your destination before you arrive can be extremely helpful. Local road signs will often direct you to parking.

NCP (National Car Parks) operates many car parks within London, as does Q-Park. Parking can be paid for in the form of "pay and display" or "phone parking". In some areas you must pay for your parking in advance. The breaking of parking rules attracts a Penalty Charge Notice (PCN) and, in certain areas, your car may be clamped and towed. Parking fines range from £80 to £130 depending on the offence. Some large shopping centres and shops have their own private parking: this may or may not be paid. Be sure to check.

Parking charges in central London during controlled hours differ on weekdays and weekends. Charges vary but can be up to £1.20 per 15 minutes in central London. Saturday prices are generally cheaper, and on Sundays there is free parking in some areas. Note that it is always forbidden to park on a double yellow line, on a red route line or on the zig zags near pedestrian crossings.

Due to all these costs, public transport is highly recommended as an alternative to driving. Most of the public transport in London is operated by one company: Transport for London.

Public Transport – The Oyster Card

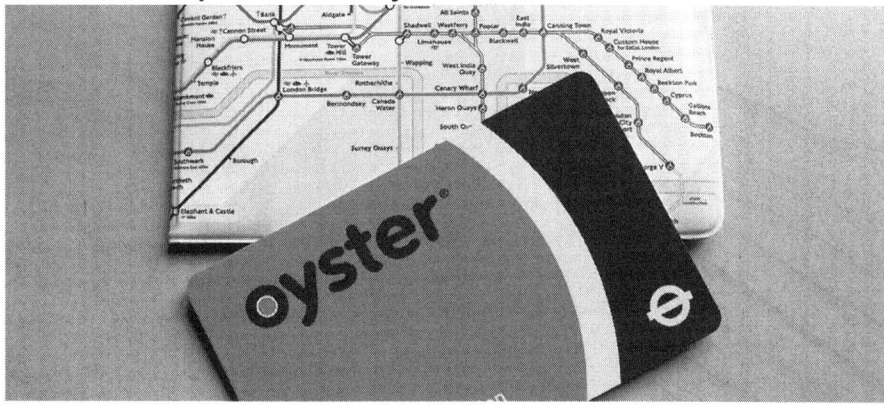

What is it?
The Oyster Card is at the heart of transportation ticketing in London. Introduced in 2003, the Oyster Card is a contactless rechargeable pre-payment smartcard that you can use instead of cash on all public transport in London.

Although cash is still accepted of most services across London (note that cash is not accepted on any London bus), over 95% of all journeys in London are made using a contactless payment method, such as the Oyster Card.

Oyster Cards eliminate the need to search for change when boarding public transport. This has made bus journeys, in particular, faster and more reliable.

Will it save me money?
An Oyster Card is a serious money saver, with big discounts over cash fares. As an example, a cash journey on the Underground in central London (zones 1 and 2) is £4.90 at any time of day. The equivalent journey paid using an Oyster Card is £2.90 at peak times and £2.40 at off-peak times. That's a saving of up to 50%!

Where can I get one?
The easiest way to get an Oyster Card, is to visit any Underground station. Oyster Cards can be purchased from ticket machines directly. There is a £5 refundable deposit for the card. You can then top it up at the ticket machines at any station, online, at Customer Service locations, as well as at independent retailers showing oyster advertising on shop windows. You can top-up your card using both cash and credit or debit cards.

Once your visit to London has ended, you can choose to either keep your Oyster Card, or get a refund. Your refund will be for all the credit left on the card (up to £10), as well as the £5 deposit you paid for the card. You can do this at certain ticket machines at Underground stations.

The Oyster card has largely replaced the paper Travelcard (see the next section) for most Londoners. This is because it is never more expensive than a paper Travelcard, and often it is much cheaper.

How do I use an Oyster Card?
On a bus, you tap your Oyster Card on the yellow reader by the driver on the way in. You do not need to do anything when leaving the bus as all bus journeys are a flat fare regardless of distance. On the Underground, Overground, National Rail services and the DLR you must tap your Oyster Card on the yellow reader on the way in (either at a ticket barrier or a standalone reader if the station has no barriers), and also on the way out to calculate the correct fare. Failure to do so will result in a penalty charge. If you only tap in or out, but not both, you will be charged a maximum journey fare.

How much is a single journey on the tube with Oyster?
Zone 1 Only – £2.40 at any time
Zones 1 and 2 – £2.90 at peak times, and £2.40 off-peak
Zones 1 to 3 – £3.30 at peak times, and £2.80 off-peak
Zones 1 to 4 – £3.90 at peak times, and £2.80 off-peak
Zones 1 to 5 – £4.70 at peak times, and £3.10 off-peak
Zones 1 to 6 – £5.10 at peak times, and £3.10 off-peak

Peak times are 06:30 to 09:30 both into and out of central London, and 16:00 to 19:00 going from central London outwards.

What is the maximum I can pay in a day?
When you travel using an Oyster Card, the system automatically sets a daily "cap". When your individual fares reach this amount, you will not be charged any further. This is the equivalent of the 1-Day Travelcard price, or cheaper.

The daily caps on Oyster Cards are:
Zone 1 Only – £6.50
Zone 1 and 2 – £6.50
Zones 1 to 3 – £7.60
Zones 1 to 4 – £9.30
Zones 1 to 5 – £11.00
Zones 1 to 6 – £11.80

Oyster Cards do not provide a weekly or 7-day cap. So, the daily cap will be applied each day. If you think you will be using your Oyster Card to the maximum value each and every day for at least 5 days in a row, then a 7-day Travelcard can be added to your Oyster Card to save money. See more in the next section.

Travelcards

A Travelcard is a 1-day, 7-day, 1-month or annual ticket which allows you unlimited travel on London Underground services, London buses, trams, National Rail services, the Overground and the DLR (Docklands Light Railway) during its validity. You can buy the Travelcard for as many zones as you like – if you will be sticking to central London, then a zone 1 and zone 2 Travelcard is sufficient.

The 1-day Travelcard can be bought as a paper ticket. The 7-day, 1-month and longer Travelcards can be added to an Oyster Card and are not available in paper form.

Unlike some other cities, such as Paris, in London when you buy a Travelcard it runs for either 7-days or a full month – not a calendar week or month, but the full amount of time from the date of purchase. For example, a 7-day travel card is valid from the current day for a week. E.g. From Tuesday until next Monday night, or Friday until next Thursday night.

The monthly Travelcard works in the same way; it does not run for a calendar month – it is a full month from the purchase date. E.g. It would run for a full month from the 17th March to 16th April. The period of validity starts immediately at the time of purchase.

Travelcard Pricing
Zone 1 to 2 – £12.10 per day, £32.40 for a week
Zones 1 to 3 – £12.10 per day, £38.00 for a week
Zones 1 to 4 – £12.10 per day, £46.50 for a week

Other options are available for additional zones. Travelcards can be bought at any London Underground ticket machine.

Contactless Travel

A relatively new addition to London is the ability to use a Contactless credit or debit card to travel on the entire Underground, Bus, Overground, Tram, National Rail and DLR network.

This means that anyone visiting London no longer needs to buy an Oyster Card or paper ticket to travel. They simply tap their contactless-enabled debit or credit card on the yellow Oyster Card readers and it will work in the same way as an Oyster Card. There is no need to top up, as the money is taken from your bank account at the end of the day.

International visitors should be aware that many banks charge fees for foreign transactions (such as those made in pounds sterling). International visitors should also inform their bank about their travel to London in advance to minimise the risk of their cards being blocked for fraud prevention reasons.

Contactless travel prices are the same as on an Oyster Card, and there is a daily cap as on Oyster. Contactless users also get the added benefit of a weekly price cap (unlike a 7-Day Travelcard, this cap is Monday to Sunday only). The weekly cap is the same price as a 7-day Travelcard.

You cannot add a Travelcard to a contactless payment card. Fares are charged as they go, until the price of a 1-day or 7-Day Travelcard are reached.

Users of the latest generations of iPhones can also use Apple Pay in the same way as a contactless payment card. Remember to have enough mobile phone battery to complete the journey or you may be charged an incomplete journey fare, or a penalty fare.

Journey Planning

As you will come to see in this section, the London transport system is vast and there are many forms of transport. However, modern technology makes it much easier to travel around London than ever before.

On the web, Transport for London's official website – ww.tfl.gov.uk – allows you to plan a journey from any station, point of interest or postcode to another within London. You can also see live bus, train and tube departure times. It will then give you the best route options. The website is also mobile-optimised for when you are on the go.

As far as smartphone apps are concerned, we highly recommend Citymapper – it has the same features as the TfL website, plus many more. It, of course, allows you to plan journeys, see live transport departures, Santander Cycling bike availability, and even includes a full tube and rail map.

However, our favorite Citymapper feature is the companion-style help that the app provides; it will help you every step of the way, even telling you when to get off a bus (using GPS), and automatically adjust your estimated arrival time. This app requires an active internet connection to plan your journey, but you can make your trip without a connection.

London Underground

The London Underground (also known as the "tube") is the world's oldest underground railway system, having first come into operation in 1863. The Underground is a constantly changing and evolving phenomenon, and has helped make London what it is today. London simply would not be the city as we know it without the Underground.

The system has grown to 270 stations, 250 miles (402km), and on a busy day the tube carries over 4.8 million passengers. Wherever you are in central London, it is never more than a 10-minute walk to a tube station, making the Underground a great way to get around.

The London Underground, Overground, National Rail, TfL Rail and Docklands Light Railway operate on Transport for London's zonal system. This categorises stations into zones depending on their distance from the centre of London. Stations in the immediate centre are in Zone 1, those furthest away are in Zone 6. The main zones are zones 1 to 6, with only a few stations in extended zones numbered 7 to 9. Zones are used to calculate fares. Crossing more zones means a higher ticket fare.

You only need to know your destination station name and staff will be able to figure out what ticket you need, but if purchasing a Travelcard it is useful to know which zones you require to minimise the cost.

If you are visiting the city centre only, Zones 1 to 2 will be where you spend most of your time. As a visitor you should rarely have to travel further than Zone 4, with most travel being done within the two central zones. It is important to note that zones do NOT apply to buses, on which there is a flat fare regardless of distance.

The London Underground is made up of eleven lines; these connect with the Overground, TfL Rail, DLR and National Rail systems.

The Underground is currently going through a huge refurbishment and upgrade program after decades of neglect, and all the trains and station are being updated. Upgrades are expected to be ongoing and continuous for the foreseeable future, with expansions and updates being planned as far in advance as 2033.

As far as accessibility is concerned, the system is far from fully accessible. This was not considered when the Underground was built over 150 years ago; advances are being made in this respect, but visitors with limited mobility should check before they travel for the best route as wheelchair access is still very limited.

The London Underground is not a 24-hour system. The first trains leave depots at approximately 5:00am, with the last trains returning to them at 1:00am. This allows for a 3- to 4-hour gap for maintenance work, depending on the location on the line. If you require an early or late train, particularly on a Sunday, do check the timetables online – on Sunday, trains start up to 90 minutes later than on weekdays, and service ends about an hour earlier than the rest of the week. There are no Transport for London services on Christmas Day. On the crossover from New Years Eve to New Years Day, the trains run all night long.

At peak times, the Underground experiences heavy overcrowding and stations are frequently temporarily closed in order to avoid the overloading of platforms. It is uncommon to board a train at peak times and find a seat. Standing room can be very limited too. The upgrade program aims to improve this through better layouts, faster trains and a more frequent train service. Capacity on some lines will increase by up to 65%. During off-peak times of the day, it is an entirely different experience and finding a seat is far from a challenge. The Underground system is clean, efficient and safe.

Due to licensing restrictions and the ever-changing nature of the London Underground map, we are unable to feature the official map of the system in this guide. Instead, we recommend you download the PDF map of the underground from **http://content.tfl.gov.uk/standard-tube-map.pdf**. This does not include National Rail services, but does include the Overground, TfL Rail and the DLR.

We recommend you have this available on a tablet where you can pinch and zoom to view the map or print it out to at least A4 size. Printed maps can also be obtained at Underground station at no cost.

Night Tube
The Mayor of London has been working hard to implement a Night Tube option. This was due to be introduced in September 2015. However, as of January 2016, the trade unions have refused to implement this service. We hope that this service will eventually be able to run. If this service is introduced, it would run on Friday and Saturday nights throughout the night. Trains would run on the entirety of the Jubilee and Victoria lines, and selected routes on the Northern, Piccadilly and Central Lines, at intervals of every 8 to 20 minutes.

Wi-Fi Access on the Underground
Over 250 Underground stations, including entrance halls, platforms and escalators have Wi-Fi access provided by Virgin Media. The speeds available are incredible. There is no Wi-Fi onboard the London Underground trains themselves or in the tunnels between stations. Customers of Virgin Media (broadband or mobile phone), EE, Three, O2 and Vodafone get free access to this Wi-Fi. Other passengers may purchase a Wi-Fi pass access directly on their device by connecting to the network. All passengers can connect and see the status of the tube lines without having to buy a Wi-Fi pass.

Buses

Buses are a fantastic way to get around London, with dedicated bus lanes meaning that in many cases a journey on a bus is quicker than the equivalent journey by car. London's buses are clean, efficient, and are fully accessible to wheelchair users, and include audio and visual announcements for each stop too.

All buses in London are cashless – this means that you must use either an Oyster Card or a contactless payment card to board. A Day Travelcard or a One-Day Bus & Tram Pass can also be used to board a bus – these can be purchased at any tube station in paper ticket form or added to an Oyster Card.

The fare for one journey is £1.50. A One-Day Bus & Tram pass is £5.00, however if you use Contactless or Oyster Pay as You Go, then the price cap is £4.50, making this better value than the day pass. If you run out of money on your Oyster Card, you will be able make "one more journey" and your card will dip into a negative balance. This must be repaid next time when topping up.

For those on a budget, the £4.50 price cap for bus-only travel on Oyster Cards offers fantastic value for money.

You can check the time of your next bus either through electronic 'countdown' signs at bus stops, or by following the text message instructions posted at bus stops. Printed timetables and schedules are also available at bus stops.

Most bus routes in central London have a frequency of every 10 minutes or less; on Sundays, this wait doubles to 'up to' every 20 minutes on Sundays.

The section below lists some of the most notable locations on central London's key bus routes. Grab a seat up top and make your own bus tour.

Key Central London Bus Routes:
* Route 8 – Shoreditch High Street, Liverpool Street, Bank, Chancery Lane, Holborn and Tottenham Court Road
* Route 9 – Aldwych, Trafalgar Square, Pall Mall (St. James's Palace), Green Park, Knightsbridge, Royal Albert Hall and High Street Kensington
* Route 10 – King's Cross, St Pancras, Euston, Tottenham Court Road, Oxford Street, Oxford Circus, Bond Street, Marble Arch, Knightsbridge, Royal Albert Hall and High Street Kensington
* Route 11 – Shoreditch High Street, Bank, St Paul's Cathedral, Fleet Street, Trafalgar Square, Westminster, Victoria and Sloane Square
* Route 14 – Euston Square, Tottenham Court Road, Shaftesbury Avenue, Piccadilly Circus, Green Park, Knightsbridge and South Kensington
* Route 15 – Aldgate, Tower Hill (Tower of London), Monument, St Paul's Cathedral, Fleet Street and Trafalgar Square
* Route 23 – Liverpool Street, Bank, St Paul's Cathedral, Trafalgar Square, Piccadilly Circus, Oxford Circus, Bond Street, Marble Arch, Edgware Road and Paddington
* Route 24 – Camden Town, Euston Square, Tottenham Court Road, Leicester Square, Trafalgar Square and Westminster
* Route 38 – Bloomsbury Way (British Museum), Shaftesbury Avenue, Piccadilly Circus, Green Park, Hyde Park Corner and Victoria
* Route 59 – St Pancras, Russell Square, Aldwych, Waterloo and Kennington Road (Imperial War Museum)
* Route 73 – Kings Cross, St Pancras, Euston, Oxford Street, Park Lane, Hyde Park Corner and Victoria
* Route 74 – South Kensington, Knightsbridge and Marble Arch
* Route 139 – Abbey Road, Baker Street, Oxford Circus, Piccadilly Circus, Trafalgar Square and Waterloo
* Route 274 – Camden Town, London Zoo, Lord's Cricket Ground and Marble Arch
* Route C2 – Victoria, Green Park, Oxford Circus and Albany Street (for London Zoo)
* Route RV1 – Covent Garden, Aldwych, Waterloo, London Eye, Tate Modern, London Bridge, Tower Bridge and Tower of London

Transport for London provides these key routes, and some others, in the form of a well-designed map. You can download the latest version at **http://content.tfl.gov.uk/bus-route-maps/key-bus-routes-in-central-london.pdf**

Overground and Dockland Light Railway (DLR)

The London Overground is operated by Transport for London and works in a very similar manner to the London Underground. The routes are featured on the London Underground map and they should be treated the same as any underground line, except that these run mostly above the surface. Most visitors to London will not make use of the Overground as it is mainly an orbital railway linking London's suburbs.

The Dockland Light Railway is a light rail system connecting the east of London and parts of central London. The trains are all computer operated and provide some great views of Canary Wharf (one of London's banking districts). Again, most visitors to London are unlikely to use the DLR. If you are visiting Stratford (for the shopping centre and the Olympic Park), Greenwich (for the Cutty Sark, the museums and the observatory), Bank and Tower Hill (for the Tower of London), then the DLR is an efficient and pleasant way to travel.

Oyster Cards, contactless payment cards and paper tickets work in the same way on both the Overground and DLR as they do on the London Underground. One thing to be aware of is that on both the Overground and the DLR, many stations do not have ticket barriers and instead have standalone card readers on the platforms or by station entrances – remember to tap your Oyster Card or contactless payment card before you board a train in order to pay the correct fare and to avoid being charge a fine.

A good number of the Overground stations are accessible to wheelchair users. All DLR stations are fully accessible to wheelchair users from the street directly onto the train.

Wi-Fi on the Overground

Over 70 Overground stations provide Wi-Fi access. As with the London Underground, Wi-Fi on the Overground is not available on the trains, but merely at the stations themselves. Access is free to everyone, provided by The Cloud.

TfL Rail (Soon to be Elizabeth Line)

TfL Rail is a relatively new addition to the London network of services. Up until 2015, it was a National Rail service, though it has now been taken over by Transport for London.

'TfL Rail' is the temporary name for a section of a huge new underground rail line that is being built – the Elizabeth Line – which will open in phases from May 2017 to December 2019. In total it will add 10% more rail capacity to the capital and dramatically speed up journeys.

At the moment, TfL Rail is essentially just a rebranded national rail service but when fully operational Elizabeth Line will link east and west London, as well as commuting towns outside of London. Ticketing works in the same way as on the Underground (Oyster, Contactless and paper tickets) and stations will be integrated with the Underground and Overground networks.

The section that is operating at the time of writing, in 2016, runs from Liverpool Street in central London, out towards Stratford in the east, and all the way to Shenfield well outside the city.

Travelers from Heathrow Airport will be particularly pleased to hear that the airport will be one of the stops on the line, connecting many places in central London and drastically reducing journey times. This is because The Elizabeth Line will take over the 'Heathrow Connect' lines. Heathrow Terminal 1, 2, 3 to Paddington will only take 23 minutes on Crossrail, versus 27 minutes currently on the Heathrow Connect today, and 15 minutes on the Heathrow Express.

Crossrail will also stop at Heathrow Terminal 4, but not at Terminal 5. You will need to change to the Piccadilly line for the last stop.

To give you another example of how journey times will improve. Bond Street will only be 26 minutes from Heathrow, as opposed to 51 minutes today. Crossrail will bring big benefits to London. The Heathrow to Paddington section of the line will open in May 2018.

National Rail

The final part of the London public transport system is National Rail trains. These are mainly commuter services that come from the suburbs into London, and from across the UK. They are not operated by Transport for London; each major commuting line is run by a different Train Operating Company. National Rail services are exceptionally busy during the morning and evening peak.

You can buy a paper ticket, use an Oyster Card or a Contactless payment card to board all National Rail services within London zones 1 to 9, and certain other stations. Since January 2016, you can also now use Oyster Cards and Contactless payments on National Rail services to and from Gatwick Airport, including the Gatwick Express.

One of the most impressive National Rail journeys is the Southeastern High Speed service (previously dubbed the "javelin" during the 2012 London Olympics) from St. Pancras International to Stratford International (for the Olympic Park). This journey takes a mere 6 minutes on this train. The comparable Underground and DLR journey takes 27 minutes (with several changes), and the bus journey takes 1 hour 25 minutes.

Oyster Cards and Contactless payments are not valid on the Heathrow Express, and the Heathrow Connect between Hayes & Harlington and Heathrow. They are also not accepted on East Midlands Trains, Grand Central, Hull Trains, Virgin Trains, or Virgin Trains East Coast services – these trains do not stop within London anyway, they are services to cities and towns outside the UK which start in London. For these journeys paper tickets are required.

Cycling

One of the cheapest and best ways to get around London is on a bike. Cycling has become a huge phenomenon in London over the past 10 years, and many commuters now use it as their main form of travel.
Cycling is allowed on all roads, you may not ride on the pavement, and some parks have specially designated cycle lanes – you must not ride outside these lanes.

In the UK, wearing a helmet is not legally required but we strongly recommend it.

Santander Cycles

In 2010, London got its first large-scale public bike hire scheme, now known as Santander Cycles. The bikes are commonly called by Londoners 'Boris Bikes' after the then Mayor of London, Boris Johnson, who fought for the scheme. The service was previously known as Barclays Cycle Hire until Summer 2015 when the sponsor changed. The scheme has 10,000 bicycles for rental and there are 700 docking stations, each with many spaces to rent or drop off a bike.

You simply walk up to any cycle docking station with an available bike (these are located every 300m to 500m), insert your credit or debit card into the payment terminal and select the number of bikes you would like to hire. Then, you will be given a code on a receipt. Go to the bike, tap in the code onto the keypad next to the bike and the bike will be released. Simply ride around and then return it to any docking point around the city.

The scheme offers good value for money for those who use it right. Fees are split into two parts: an access charge and a journey charge. The daily access price is £2 for a 24-hour pass. This access charge allows you to make as many journeys as you wish, each lasting 30 minutes or less, during the 24-hour period with no extra fee to pay. If you make a journey that lasts over 30 minutes, there is an additional journey charge, which is £2 per 30 minutes.

The idea is that you use the bike to go between places and not to continuously ride around all day. This ensures that there are always bikes in circulation. If you have a journey that is longer than 30 minutes (this would astound us if you are just sightseeing), then you can split your journey before you get to the 30-minute mark and wait five minutes between hires to avoid this.

When returning a bike, if you reach a docking station with no free bike spaces, simply go to the terminal at the docking station and click the button that says "No docking point free". Follow the on-screen instructions. This will tell you where there are free spaces nearby, and grant you 15 extra minutes to make this journey.

For visitors to the city who want to keep fit and save money, whilst also getting around relatively quickly, this scheme is perfect. The bikes are available 24 hours a day, 7 days a week. Get the official smartphone app to see the availability and location of docking stations updated in real time.

Cycle Lanes and Cycle Superhighways

As cycling has become so popular in recent years, cycle lanes have become increasingly common in London, particularly in the central area. When a cycle lane is available, cyclists should stick to it, as it is usually the safest option. Cycle lanes are commonly located next to bus lanes, and cyclists should be particularly wary of left-turning traffic when riding.

The city is also building and upgrading London Cycle Superhighways. Older versions share the road space with existing vehicles with a bike lane painted onto the road; newer Superhighways are completely segregated from traffic with a dedicated cycling area. These separated schemes should make cycling in these areas much safer and more pleasant.

River Services

River Services are yet another form of public transport in London. These take the form of scenic sightseeing river cruises (with commentary), and river taxi services (without commentary). The Mayor of London wishes to expand these services in coming years.

Thames Clippers runs the river boat services in London. The five routes that currently run are limited in scope. The most commonly used route for visitors will be RB1 which links the London Eye going eastwards towards Embankment, Blackfriars, London Bridge, Tower Bridge, Canary Wharf, Greenwich and North Greenwich (for The O2). Four other lines are available but RB1 is the most comprehensive.

River services operate every 20 to 30 minutes on all lines, and the boats have onboard cafes, bars and seating. Most boats also have onboard toilets. Journeys take about 17 minutes from the London Eye to Tower Pier, and 45 minutes from the London Eye to The O2. All passengers are guaranteed a seat by law.

Pricing
Fares for the river services are expensive compared to the rest of London's public transport network. If you buy your tickets at ticket offices, adult single fares vary between £4.20 and £8.20 depending on the distance travelled. A River Roamer day ticket (unlimited travel in Central and East areas from 9:00am) is £17.35. Children 5 to 15 pay half price. Under 5s travel free.

If you buy your ticket in advance online, use an Oyster Card (Pay as You Go) or buy tickets on the Thames Clipper app, prices are cheaper - £3.90 to £7.20 for a single ticket, and £14.70 for a River Roamer (the River Roamer is online only). Contactless payment card travel is not yet available at the time of writing.

Travelcards (both paper on Oyster) are not valid on river services but you will receive a 30% discount off your river ticket or pass.

Top Tip: These are commuter boats and not designed for visitors as they have no board commentary. However, Thames Clipper has created an audio guide for your journey that works using the GPS on your phone. The app is called "Thames Clippers in:flow", and is available for free on both Apple and Android devices.

Tramlink

If you venture into South London, towards Wimbledon for example, you may come across London Tramlink – a small tram system. To be perfectly honest we cannot see why a visitor to London would use this Tramlink. The system is designed for local residents more than visitors in reality, and travels through some of the more rundown parts of London.

The tram system functions in much the same way as buses do in London. The fare is £1.50 with an Oyster Card or contactless payment card. The drivers of the trams do not sell tickets onboard, but (unlike buses) you *can* buy a cash ticket from a ticket machine at any of the tram stops.

You must touch in your Oyster Card or contactless payment card at one of the readers before boarding the tram – do not touch out when you leave, except at Wimbledon where you must do this to get through the ticket barriers.

The daily price cap is £4.50 if using Oyster. A One Day Bus & Tram Pass can also be purchased for £5. If you have a Travelcard on your Oyster card or a paper Day Travelcard that includes Zone 3, 4, 5 or 6, you can use it to travel on all trams. This is also the case, if you have a Bus & Tram Pass on your Oyster card or in paper form.

Taxis

Taxis are another popular way to get around the capital and in many cases can be the quickest journey from A-to-B within central London. Taxis (also known as Black Cabs) are allowed to use bus lanes which frequently makes them quicker than driving. There is also no parking, Congestion Charge or fuel costs to worry about.

How do I hail a cab?
Black cabs are available to hail in London by sticking your arm out in the road. Do not shout out 'Taxi'. You should only hail cabs that have the "Taxi" light switched as these are available. Those with the light switched off are already hired.

You can also find cabs at taxi ranks throughout the city – these are especially common outside airports and rail stations.

Black cabs can be pre-booked in advance through one of many taxi firms. Well known firms include Dial-a-Cab (0207 253 5000) and Radio Taxis (0207 272 0272), but many other companies are also available.

Finally, the technological elite may prefer to book a black cab through an app – Hailo and Gett are the biggest ones out there.

What training do the drivers go through?
London cab drivers go through a rigorous test called The Knowledge. They must know every street within 6 miles (10km) of Charing Cross in central London – there are over 25,000 of these, as well as all the landmarks and the quickest way to get you there. Most people take three years to pass this test. Generally speaking, cab drivers are very friendly and happy to help you out with recommendations and any questions you may have.

How much do London cabs cost?
Transport for London sets the pricing for all London taxis. Below is their pricing grid:

Distance	Approx journey time	Monday to Friday 06:00 - 20:00 (Tariff 1)	Monday to Friday 20:00 - 22:00 Saturday and Sunday 06:00 - 22:00 (Tariff 2)	Every night 22:00 - 06:00 Public holidays (Tariff 3)
1 mile	6 - 13 mins	£5.60 - £8.80	£5.60 - £9	£6.80 - £9
2 miles	10 - 20 mins	£8.60 - £13.80	£9.00 - £14	£10.40 - £14.80
4 miles	16 - 30 mins	£15 - £22	£16 - £22	£18 - £28
6 miles	28 - 40 mins	£23 - £29	£28 - £32	£28 - £33
Between Heathrow and Central London	30 - 60 mins	£45 - £85	£45 - £85	£45 - £85

Taxi journeys are priced using a mixture of journey length and journey time. The minimum fare is £2.40.

Passengers will pay the metered fare, unless a set fare has been agreed at the start of the journey – set fares are rare in London cabs. As far as tipping is concerned, rounding to the nearest £1 or £5, is common practice.

All taxis accept cash, and some accept debit and credit card payments – if you are not paying by cash, do ask this question before getting in. A surcharge is often added for card payments; this can be a maximum of £1 or 10% of the fare (whichever is higher).

The acceptance of card payments (including Contactless) in all black cabs will be mandatory from October 2016 – there will also be no card payment surcharge from this date. The minimum fare will rise from £2.40 to £2.60 at the same time.

Emirates Air Line

The Emirates Air Line, opened in 2012, has been dubbed as more of a vanity project in recent years than a form of transportation. It is a cable car system in East London that provides views of the surrounding area, as well as a link between North Greenwich (for the O2) and Royal Victoria station on the DLR. It is a unique way to see London but unless you are already in the area, we wouldn't make a special trip for it. The Air Line is subject to weather conditions.

Crossings take 5 minutes during the rush hour peak of 7:00 to 9:00, 10 minutes from 9:00 to 19:00, and Night Flights are 12 to 13 minutes after 19:00. Cabins arrive every 15 to 30 seconds and can fit up to 10 people.

The Air Line begins operation at 07:00 Monday to Friday, 08:00 on Saturday and 09:00 on Sunday. Closing times are 21:00 daily, except Friday and Saturday when the Air Line closes at 23:00. During Summer (April to September) closing times may be extended.

Fares are £4.50 for a single journey if paid by cash, and £3.50 if paid using an Oyster Card with Pay as You Go credit, or a contactless payment card. Return fares are double the single fare. Child fares are half price. Pay as You Go fares do not count towards the Oyster daily cap.

For a more serene tour (with a return journey) check out the Discovery Experience which includes in-flight audio and video, as well as a souvenir guide and entrance to the nearby Emirates Aviation Experience. The Discovery Experience is priced at £10.70 for adults or £8.40; child prices are £6.20 and £5.00 respectively.

Night Flights (after 19:00) with on-board include music and video are the same price as a standard daytime ticket.

At a Glance: Top 10 Must-See Attractions

London has hundreds of different things you can do and see, but it is likely you will only have a limited amount of time to visit the city. This section allows you to take a trip through our favourite attractions in London.

As will become apparent as you read this guide, there are a wealth of attractions on offer, including many with no admission charge.

To ease your planning, each attraction has a short description, as well as the nearest public transport links, the entry price (if applicable) and opening hours. In the chapters that follow, we also include more detailed coverage of all these attractions.

Admission prices stated are 'on-the-door' rates, and cheaper tickets can be obtained by booking in advance online, or from other sources.

Museums and galleries that are listed as providing free admission are completely free of charge, without the need to obtain a ticket. However, a donation on the way out, or a small purchase from the gift shop of one of these locations is appreciated.

Remember that popular locations may have long queue lines to get in during busier periods of the year.

Many attractions have variable opening times depending on the day of the week, the month of the year, and whether it is term time or school holidays.

To avoid disappointment, we recommend you check the opening times and dates with each attraction prior to your visit.

1. Tower of London

Nearest Station: Tower Hill and Tower Gateway
Entry price: Adult – £24.50, Child (5 to 15) – £11, Concession – £18.70. A family ticket is priced at £60.70.
Typical opening hours: On Tuesdays to Saturdays, 09:00 to 17:30 from March to October, and 09:00 to 16:30 from November to February. The attraction opens at 10:00 on Sundays and Mondays year-round.
Phone: 0203 166 6000
Website: www.hrp.org.uk/tower-of-london/

Of all the major tourist attractions in London to visit, the Tower of London is undoubtedly our favourite. It is amazing to see this castle, constructed in 1078, still standing in the very heart of London today. When first built, the Tower of London was just the 'White Tower', which currently stands in the centre of the site.

Most of the Tower of London is self-guided, but we recommend you begin your visit with one of the tours held by Yeoman Warders or 'Beefeaters'. Throughout the tour, you will get a whirlwind look at the gruesome history of the Tower and visit some of the key locations throughout the site.

Once you have finished the tour, it is time to explore the rest of the site. Every direction you go in there are intriguing exhibitions to visit. You can also walk across the top of the castle's walls, see The Queen's Crown Jewels up close, and learn about the history of the Tower from execuritons to traitors. A minimum of three to four hours is needed for a good overview of the Tower.

2. Houses of Parliament & Big Ben

Nearest Station: Westminster
Entry price: Guided Tours: Adults – £25.50, Child (5 to 15) – £11, Concessions – £21. Audio Tours: Adults – £18.50, Child – £7.50 (one free child per paying adult), Concessions – £16.
Typical opening hours: Open Saturdays throughout the year and on most weekdays during Parliamentary recesses including Christmas, Easter and the summer. English tours depart every 15 to 20 minutes from 09:00 to 16:15.
Phone: 0207 219 4114
Website: www.parliament.uk/visiting/

The home of the UK government for over 500 years, the Houses of Parliament are world-renowned. The current building dates from the 1840s; the previous building was destroyed a large fire. The most famous part of the building is undoubtedly the clock tower which lies on its northern side, largely referred to as Big Ben. However, Big Ben is actually the name of the 13.5-ton bell located inside the tower. The tower itself is called the Elizabeth Tower.

Paid tours of the inside of the building are available and advanced reservations are strongly recommended. Tours are available on Saturdays year-round, and weekdays when Parliament is in recess. Guided tours and audio tours are available, and we highly recommend them. Audio tours are available in a variety of languages, whereas Guided Tours are in English only.

The Houses of Parliament and Big Ben have become trademark symbols for London and are daily staples in films, TV shows, documentaries and news programmes around the world.

3. Hyde Park and Kensington Gardens

Nearest Stations: Marble Arch, Hyde Park Corner, Knightsbridge, Lancaster Gate, Paddington and Queensway
Entry price: Free
Typical opening hours: 05:00 to 0:00 year-round for Hyde Park. 06:00 to dusk (between 16:15 to 21:45) for Kensington Gardens.
Website: www.royalparks.org.uk/parks/

Once Henry VIII's hunting grounds, today these two green areas combine to make the largest royal park in central London, spanning some 625 acres. Today, the two parks blend almost seamlessly and offer many things to see and do.

Inside, admire The Serpentine, the largest manmade lake in London, The Princess Diana Memorial Fountain, and the Memorial Playground, and the Italian Gardens and Fountains in Kensington Gardens. Many statues, fountains and memorials are also dotted around both parks. On the western end of the Park you will also find the Royal Albert Hall, as well as Kensington Palace.

Speakers Corner on the north-east corner of the park, and closest to Marble Arch, is also another notable attraction.

4. Natural History Museum

Nearest Station: South Kensington
Entry price: Free admission
Typical opening hours: Open daily from 10:00 to 17:50. Last entry at 17:30.
Phone: 0207 942 5000
Website: www.nhm.ac.uk

The Natural History Museum is incredible popular, featuring a wide variety of permanent exhibitions in its collection. Throughout your visit you can go from marveling dinosaur skeletons and an animatronic T-Rex, to geological finds, to the enormous Mammals area, and even walk past scientists working at the museum's Darwin Centre.

The museum also offers fascinating temporary exhibitions, which are paid admission, as well as special events such as a 'Night at the Museum'-style sleepover, and after-hours "lates" events.

5. Science Museum

Nearest Station: South Kensington
Entry price: Donation based – £5 suggested
Typical opening hours: Open daily from 10:00 to 18:00. The museum closes at 19:00 during school holidays.
Phone: 0207 942 4000
Website: www.sciencemuseum.org.uk

At the Science Museum you can learn all about outer space and moon landings, take part in interactive exhibitions, see how steam trains and airplanes have revolutionised transport and much more. A whole area dedicated to young children with shows and interactive exhibitions means that learning can be fun too.

You can also find an IMAX screen showing scientific movies, as well as a simulator attraction and numerous kids play areas. Temporary exhibitions and special events mean there are always a multitude of reasons to keep coming back.

6. London Eye

Nearest Station: Waterloo
Entry price: Adult – £23.50, Child (4 to 15) – £17.50, Senior – £21.
Typical opening hours: Open daily from 10:00 to 20:30 year round, with closing times extended to between 21:30 and 23:30 during peak periods.
Phone: 0333 321 2001
Website: www.londoneye.com

For a unique view of London, step into one of the magnificent viewing capsules on the 135-metre (443 feet) tall London Eye. It is the world's tallest cantilevered Ferris wheel and from the top, you can see up to 40km on a clear day.

The London Eye's 32 capsules are constantly rotating and a journey onboard lasts 30 minutes. On board you can gaze across London, have a quick break on the seats in the middle of the capsules, or use one of the onboard tablets to learn about the monuments around you.

The London Eye experience can also be personalised to something even more special with the option of a private capsule for a couple or a group, a champagne experience, as well as other options.

Note: Every year in January, the London Eye shuts for its annual maintenance. This usually takes place during the second and third weeks of the month.

7. Trafalgar Square and The National Gallery

Nearest Station: Charing Cross
Entry price: Free admission to both Trafalgar Square and The National Gallery
Typical opening hours: National Gallery – 10:00 to 18:00 (daily) and 10:00 to 21:00 (Fridays). Closed 1st January and 24th to 26th December.
Phone: 0207 747 2885
Website: www.nationalgallery.org.uk

Trafalgar Square is a magnificent space which celebrates Lord Admiral Horatio Nelson's victory in 1805 against the French and Spanish forces at Cape Trafalgar. Nelson's Column dominates the square, standing at 135 feet tall – the same height as his ship (the HMS Victory). Atop of the column is an 18-foot statue of Nelson himself.

Notable buildings around Trafalgar Square include:
* The National Gallery, a free admission museum which houses priceless works of art including Van Gogh's 'Sunflowers' and Monet's 'Waterlillies' amongst many others. The paintings on offer cover several centuries, and even the building's interior architecture is worth admiring. The paid-for audio guide is thoroughly recommended. The National Gallery also has a paid-for 'Sainsbury Wing', which features temporary exhibitions and collections.
* The Canadian, South African, and Ugandan High Commissions line the square.
* St. Martin in the Fields Church, located to the right of The National Gallery is the church where royal births are registered. It is famous for its Crypt Café which serves warm food at pub-friendly prices in a beautiful underground setting.
* The National Portrait Gallery is also just off the square, and features portraits of famous figures from British history.

8. The British Museum

Nearest Station: Russell Square, Holborn and Tottenham Court Road
Entry price: Free
Typical opening hours: 10:00 to 17:30 (daily) and 10:00 to 20:30 (Fridays)
Phone: 0207 323 8299
Website: www.britishmuseum.org

The British Museum is one of the largest museums in the world and houses over seven million artifacts relating to human history and culture. One of the most fascinating items on display is the Rosetta Stone, which was the key to us understanding Egyptian hieroglyphics. The cat mummies are also fascinating, as are the Egyptian sarcophagi, also on display.

There are also regular rotating free and paid exhibitions, which mean that each visit to this magnificent place is different and equally fascinating.

9. West End – Piccadilly Circus & Leicester Square

Nearest Station: Piccadilly Circus and Leicester Square
Entry price: Free – Public area

The West End is one of the busiest and liveliest areas of London. Although, there is a whole sections dedicated to the West End in the neighbourhood guide section of this book, we would like to pinpoint both Piccadilly Circus and Leicester Square as the heart of the area.

Piccadilly Circus anchors one side of the West End with the famous Piccadilly Lights, the giant advertising billboards. The first of these was put up back in 1908, and was the world's first set of outdoor electric lights. They have been upgraded over the years and are now only on one corner of the Circus area.

Also in the area, are the Statue of Anteros and the Shaftsbury fountain dedicated to the 7th Earl of Shaftesbury who fought to stop children becoming chimneysweeps. Anteros is The Angel of Christian Charity, but is often mistaken for Eros – the Greek god of love.

Chinatown is also a short walk away from Piccadilly Circus down Shaftsbury Avenue. Moving towards Haymarket you can see the Horses of Helios and The Three Graces (Helios' daughters).

Continuing towards Leicester Square, you can enjoy the multitude of souvenir shops available here, as well as the cinemas where film premieres are regularly held. TKTS is also present on the square, which sells half price theatre tickets for many shows on the day of performance.

10. Buckingham Palace

Nearest Station: St. James's Park and Victoria
Entry price: See neighbourhood guide.
Typical opening hours: See neighbourhood guide.
Website: www.royal.gov.uk/theroyalresidences/buckinghampalace/

Home of the monarch since Queen Victoria made it her residence in 1837, Buckingham Palace has become a true icon of London. From the famous balcony to the iconic guards and the golden Victoria statue and fountain, Buckingham Palace is a sight not to be missed.

From the Changing the Guard ceremony, to tours of the inside the of the palace, there are a multitude of ways to enjoy this magnificent place.

Note that no bus tours or London bus routes pass by the 'front' of Buckingham Palace where the balcony is located, due to traffic restrictions. Bus tours will stop on the side of the palace and passengers can hop off and make their way round.

Neighbourhood Guides: London Area by Area

London is split up into 32 boroughs, plus The City of London area in the centre. We think that the listing of boroughs, however, is a bit of an arcane way to look at London when visiting it.

Instead, we have split the main areas in the centre of London into neighbourhoods. These are:
* Westminster, Victoria & St. James's
* The Southbank
* West End and Trafalgar Square
* Kensington & The Museums
* The City
* London Bridge
* Hyde Park, Notting Hill & Bayswater
* Marylebone, Bloomsbury and Camden
* Further Afield – Attractions outside central London

Below is a very simple diagram of where these different areas are located in central London.

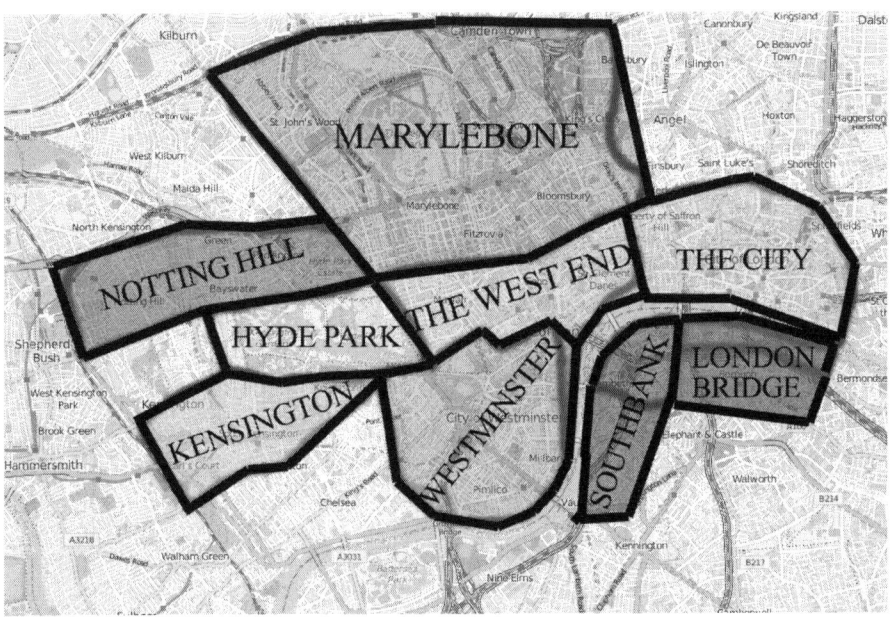

Each of these areas is unique in character, from areas filled with art galleries and theatres, to residential areas. All of them are worth exploring.

We highly recommend you begin your trip planning by reading through all of this section and bookmarking the attractions you would like to see and the restaurants you would like to eat in. We also list accommodation options for each area allowing you to choose somewhere that fits your taste and budget best.

Concession prices listed in this section usually apply to over 60s or over 65s (proof may be requested), and students on production of a valid student ID.

Attraction opening times are pretty standard year-round but you should be especially wary of opening times from 24th to 26th December, and on 31st December and 1st January. Some locations do not open at all on these dates, and others operate restricted opening hours. Some locations may also not open on bank holidays or fixed days each week.

We also list the closest underground station to each listing. Where there are multiple listings for the nearest station, the first listed is the closest and/or most convenient to the attraction.

Note that reviews in this section are opinions, and not facts. Your mileage may vary with attractions, accommodation and dining locations.

Westminster, Victoria & St. James's

Westminster is well known for being the home of the UK government, with the Houses of Parliament being where debates are held. There are also countless governmental buildings down Whitehall. Westminster is also well known for the large Abbey which is the location of coronations, and was where the Royal Wedding between Kate Middleton and Prince William took place a few years ago.

Immediately next door are the areas of Victoria and St. James's where Buckingham Palace is located, as well as the busy Victoria Station. Victoria is home to a lot of accommodation for both locals and visitors alike. The area was largely just fields until Queen Victoria moved into Buckingham Palace in 1837, and the development of the area began.

Attractions
Buckingham Palace

Nearest Stations: St. James's Park and Victoria
Address: Buckingham Palace Rd, London, SW1A 1AA
Entry price: £21.50 adults, £12.30 for under-17s, £19.60 for concessions.
Typical opening hours: See description.
Website: www.royal.gov.uk/theroyalresidences/buckinghampalace/

Home of the monarch since Queen Victoria made it her residence in 1837, Buckingham Palace has become a true icon of London. From the famous balcony to the iconic guards, and the golden Victoria memorial statue to the imposing fountain, Buckingham Palace is a sight not to be missed.

The 'Changing the Guard' ceremony is one of the main attractions of the palace where you can see the royal guards marching to the palace to replace another regiment, accompanied by a band. The guard change ceremony happens every day from April to the end of July, and every other day during the rest of the year – check ahead for times around Christmas and New Year too, as these dates rarely follow the rest of the month's schedule. Although the ceremony reaches its height at around 11:30am at Buckingham Palace, you will want to be there at least 45 minutes before to get a good spot.

Access inside the palace is strictly restricted. For most of the year you cannot access the interior of Buckingham Palace itself, but can instead visit The Royal Mews, and The Queen's Gallery throughout the year. During Winter, usually from December to January, there are exclusive guided tours available to reserve.

Furthermore, during select dates in the Summer, the nineteen State Rooms of the palace are available to visit, as well as the gardens in a self-guided tour. A visit to the State Rooms will last about two hours total once you are inside. In 2016, the State Rooms are open to visitors from 30th July to 25th September inclusive.

One generous advantage of a ticket to Buckingham Palace's grounds is that any tickets bought directly allow free re-admission for a year if you get them stamped on the way out. This is one of our favourite things to do in all of London.

The Queen's Gallery
Nearest Stations: St. James's Park and Victoria
Address: Buckingham Palace Rd, London SW1A 1AA
Entry price: £10 adults, £5.20 for under-17s, £9.20 for concessions.
Typical opening hours: Open daily from 10:00 to 17:30 year-round. Opens at 9:30 from 30th July to 25th September 2015.
Website: www.royalcollection.org.uk/visit/the-queens-gallery-buckingham-palace

This gallery showcases a constantly rotating series of works from the Royal Collection. Over 450 works can be seen at any one time. Be sure to check for what the latest exhibition is before visiting.

Tickets for this attraction can be combined with those for The Royal Mews and even Buckingham Palace's state room tours for savings.

The Royal Mews

Nearest Stations: St. James's Park and Victoria
Address: Buckingham Palace Rd, London SW1A 1AA
Entry price: £9.30 adults, £5.50 for under-17s, £8.50 for concessions.
Typical opening hours: Open daily from 10:00 to 17:00 during late March to October, and Monday to Saturday from 10:00 to 16:00 during February to March, and November.
Website: www.royalcollection.org.uk/visit/royalmews

Located in Buckingham Palace's grounds, and open for the majority of the year, the Royal Mews is a working stable where you can see traditional coaches and carriages used in royal ceremonial occasions, as well as the horses themselves. The Diamond Jubilee State Coach on display is particularly stunning.

Furthermore, between April and October a 45-minute guided tour is available, and included in the price of your ticket. This showcases the highlights of the Royal Mews as you are accompanied by one of Buckingham Palace's wardens.

Clarence House

Nearest Stations: Green Park and Charing Cross
Address: Little St James's Street, St. James's, London, SW1A 1BA
Entry price: Adults and Concessions – £10, Children (5 to 16) – £6
Typical opening hours: Open 1st to 31st August 2016. Monday to Friday from 10:00 to 16:30, Saturday and Sunday from 10:00 to 17.30.
Phone: 0207 766 7303
Website: www.royalcollection.org.uk/visit/clarence-house

Clarence House is the official London residence of The Prince of Wales, The Duchess of Cornwall, and Prince Harry. The building was designed by John Nash and was completed in 1827, and is located right next door to St. James's Palace. The house was recently also home to Queen Elizabeth, The Queen Mother.

Houses of Parliament & Big Ben

Nearest Station: Westminster
Address: Houses of Parliament, Westminster, London SW1A 0AA
Entry price: Guided Tours: Adults – £25.50, Child (5 to 15) – £11, Concessions – £21. Audio Tours: Adults – £18.50, Child – £7.50 (one free child per paying adult), Concessions – £16.
Typical opening hours: Open Saturdays throughout the year and on most weekdays during Parliamentary recesses, such as Christmas, Easter and the summer. Live tours depart every 15 to 20 minutes from 09:00 to 16:15.
Phone: 0207 219 4114
Website: www.parliament.uk/visiting/

The home of the UK government for over 500 years, the Houses of Parliament are world-renowned. The current building dates from the 1840s and the previous building on the site was destroyed by a large fire in 1834 – only a very small part remains. The old Palace of Westminster that stood on this site was also unfortunately destroyed by a fire in 1512.

The most famous part of the building is undoubtedly the clock tower which lies on its northern side, largely referred to as Big Ben. However, Big Ben is actually the name of the 13.5-ton bell located inside the Elizabeth Tower. The reason behind the bell's naming is still disputed to this day, but one likely reason is that Benjamin Hall was the commissioner of works at the time the original bell was installed.

Paid tours of the inside of the building are available and advanced reservations are strongly recommended. Tours are available on Saturdays year-round, and weekdays when Parliament is in recess. The best place to check for exact opening dates and times is at **www.parliament.uk/visiting/visiting-and-tours/tours-of-parliament/**. Guided tours last approximately 90 minutes. Audio tours are also available on the same dates and are self-guided, usually lasting between 60 and 75 minutes. Both sets of tours will take you inside the beautiful Westminster Hall, the Queen's Robing Room, the Royal Gallery, the Lords and Commons Chamber, St. Stephen's Hall and many more locations. Learn about the fascinating history, as well as how the building is used as a working location today.

UK visitors may also contact their local MP, or a member of the House of Lords who they know, to request a free guided tour available year-round. UK visitor tours last 75 minutes and these are generally fully booked 6 months in advance. In addition, UK residents can tour the Elizabeth Tower and see Big Ben (the bell) up close by applying through the aforementioned methods – again these tours are very popular and are generally booked 6 months in advance.

The Houses of Parliament and Big Ben have become a trademark symbol for London and are daily staples in films, TV shows, documentaries and news programmes across the world.

The Jewel Tower

Nearest Station: Westminster
Address: Abingdon Street, Westminster, London, SW1P 3JX
Entry price: Adults – £4.20, Children (5 to 15) – £2.50, Concessions – £3.80
Typical opening hours: Winter (November to March) – Open weekends from 10:00 to 16:00, Summer (April to October) – Open daily 10:00 to 17:30
Phone: 0207 222 2219
Website: www.english-heritage.org.uk/visit/places/jewel-tower/

Built in 1365 to house Edward III's personal treasure collection, the Jewel Tower is one of the few surviving areas of the old Palace of Westminster, which was razed by a fire. Today, you can find an exhibition that spans all three floors inside and revisits the tower's numerous roles over the past 650 years, and even includes a model of the Palace of Westminster before the 1834 fire destroyed it.

Downing Street
Nearest Station: Westminster
Address: Downing St, London, SW1A 2AA

Downing Street is the heart of British Government, with number 10 being the most famous address – the Prime Minster's Office and Official Residence. Number 11 on the street is the residence of the Chancellor of the Exchequer.

The origin of the street's name comes from when it was commissioned by Sir George Downing in the 1680s on the site of Hampden House.

Downing Street is not publicly accessible and is guarded by black gates and barriers, as well as armed police officers. You may take photos from Whitehall looking into Downing Street but cannot go any closer.

St. James's Palace

Nearest Stations: Green Park and Charing Cross
Address: Marlborough Rd, London, SW1A 1BS
Phone: 0207 930 4832
Website: www.royal.gov.uk/theroyalresidences/stjamesspalace

St James's Palace was largely built during the 1530s, under the reign of Henry VIII, and has been home to monarchs for over 300 years. Interestingly, despite the fact that all monarchs since Queen Victoria have lived at Buckingham Palace, St. James's is still the monarch's official residence.

Today the palace is used primarily for charity events where members of the royal family are often present, as well as offices for many royal functions. The palace also contains the London residences of The Prince of Wales, The Princess Royal and Princess Alexandra.

Although the palace is not open to the public for visiting, it is still worth walking around the outside, particularly as it is located just down the road from Buckingham Palace.

Horse Guards Parade and The HouseHold Cavalry Museum

Nearest Stations: Charing Cross and Westminster
Address: Whitehall, London, SW1A 2AX
Entry price: Adults – £7, Children (5 to 16) and Concessions – £5
Typical opening hours: Open daily from 10:00 to 17:00 November to March, with a late closing at 18:00 from April to October
Phone: 0207 930 3070
Website: www.householdcavalrymuseum.co.uk

Horse Guards Parade is a parade ground situated off Whitehall. The Horse Guards are on duty every day from 10:00 to 16:00 here, guarding one of the official entrances to Buckingham Palace. At 16:00 every day there is the inspection and dismount ceremony, which visitors can watch free of charge; simply turn up. The Changing of the Queen's Life Guard also takes place daily on Horse Guards Parade at 11:00am (10:00am on Sundays).

This parade ground also hosts "Trooping the Colours", an annual ceremony that is conducted on the official birthday of the monarch in June. The Beating Retreat is another ceremony held here on two successive evenings in June. It was formerly the venue of major tournaments that were conducted during the reign of Henry VIII. It was once also the headquarters of the British Army and was home to the Duke of Wellington. Currently it houses the General Officer commanding the district of London in the British Army.

The Horse Guard Parade grounds are free to visit, but the museum is a paid attraction. Opening dates and prices listed above are for the museum. Inside, visitors can appreciate the work that goes into being the Queen's mounted bodyguard with a unique behind the scenes look. A multi-language self-guided multimedia tour is offered to each guest at the museum and brings the exhibits to life, as you learn about this regiment's interesting past.

Churchill War Rooms

Nearest Station: Westminster
Address: Churchill War Rooms, Clive Steps, King Charles Street, London, SW1A 2AQ
Entry price: Adult - £17.25, Child (5 to 15) – £8.60, Concessions – £13.80
Typical opening hours: Every day from 09:30 to 18:00
Phone: 0207 930 6961
Website: www.iwm.org.uk/visits/churchill-war-rooms

A fascinating museum located in an underground bunker right in the heart of Westminster. The war rooms were used by the government and Winston Churchill during the Second World War. There are living quarters, planning rooms and even the original map room, which has been left unchanged since the war ended in 1945. It is a fascinating slice of London's history.

Westminster Abbey

Nearest Station: Westminster
Address: 20 Deans Yard, London, SW1P 3PA
Entry price: Adults – £20, Children (6 to 16) – £9, Concessions – £17
Typical opening hours: Monday to Saturday from 09:30 to 15:30. Occasionally open later until 18:00. Closed to visitors on Sundays and religious holidays.
Phone: 020 7222 5152
Website: www.westminster-abbey.org

This incredible building began construction in 1245 under the appointment of Henry VIII, but previous incarnations of the church have existed on the site since 960. Over the years, several extensions were added, eventually finishing in its present form five hundred years later in 1745 with the West towers.

Westminster Abbey has been home to coronations since 1066 when William the Conqueror was crowned at the site, and has been home to no less than eleven royal weddings, including most recently Prince William and Catherine Middleton.

Inside, the abbey is a magnificent work of art and the gardens are equally worth a visit. Significant areas include the North Transept, the Sanctuary, the Cloisters, the College Garden, the Tomb of Mary (Queen of Scotts), and Poet's Corner.

Guided tours of the inside of the Abbey are available for £5 extra per person and last about 90 minutes. Multi-language audio tours are complimentary and available at the abbey entrance – alternatively there is app you can download on your smartphone.

The opening hours listed above are for visitors to the abbey. Services held at the abbey are free to all. On religious days, the Abbey is only open for services and not for visiting.

Most visitors to the abbey will spend 90 minutes to 2 hours inside. Queues are lengthy for the abbey almost year-round.

Tate Britain

Nearest Station: Pimlico
Address: Millbank, London, SW1P 4RG
Entry price: Free admission. Some temporary exhibitions require an extra fee.
Typical opening Hours: Daily from 10.00 am to 6.00pm.
Phone: 0207 887 8888
Website: www.tate.org.uk/visit/tate-britain

Marvel at one of the best art collections in the world for free. The Tate Britain houses a large collection of British art, including works from John Latham and Douglas Gordon. The gallery also contains the largest number of works by J.M.W. Turner in the world. You are sure to be inspired by the many collections on offer.

Some of our favourite pieces include "King and Queen", a bronze sculpture by Henry Moore, and the stunning "Flatford Mill ('Scene on a Navigable River')" by John Constable.

Free guided tours are offered throughout the day and last 45 minutes. Other complimentary tours and talks are also regularly held.

You can take advantage of the Tate-to-Tate riverboat service to travel to the Tate Modern if you are visiting both these museums on the same day. This is a paid riverboat service.

The Cenotaph

Nearest Station: Westminster
Address: Whitehall, London, SW1A 2AX
Typical opening hours: 24/7 – Public area

The nation's main war memorial, The Cenotaph is planted in the middle of the road in Whitehall. Flags of the United Kingdom are placed around the memorial. This is also the location where the monarch and other senior members of the royal family, as well as politicians, lay wreaths of flowers every year in a large ceremony on Remembrance Sunday (the second Sunday in November).

Banqueting House

Nearest Stations: Westminster and Charing Cross

Address: Whitehall, London, SW1A 2AX
Entry price: Adults – £6.60, Children (Under 16) – Free, Concessions – £5.50
Typical opening hours: Daily from 10:00 to 17:00
Phone: 0203 166 6000
Website: www.hrp.org.uk/banqueting-house

Banqueting House is the only surviving part of the old Whitehall Palace which once spanned the entire length of the road now called Whitehall. Almost all of Whitehall Palace burnt down during a large fire in 1698 and only Banqueting House remains.

From the art and sculptures, to the stunning interiors, and even the site of King Charles I's execution, Banqueting House is definitely worth a visit.

Each year, on 30th January a service in Banqueting House remembers the execution of King Charles I.

The Battle of Britain London Monument

Nearest Station: Westminster
Address: Victoria Embankment, London, SW1A 2JH (near Big Ben's clock tower)
Entry price: Free
Typical opening hours: 24/7 – Public area
Website: www.bbm.org.uk

This stunning memorial is a beautiful gem that many people miss. Unveiled in 2005, the monument includes incredibly lifelike bronze depictions of the airmen in the 1940 battle. The way that movement has been captured is simply incredible.

The monument also contains plaques remembering the 3000 airmen and allies who fought in the battle.

It is also less than a minute's walk to the Royal Air Force Memorial located further up the Victoria Embankment.

Westminster Cathedral

Nearest Station: Victoria
Address: 42 Francis Street, London, SW1P 1QW
Entry price: Free admission to services. Tower Viewing Gallery: Adults – £6, Concessions – £4. Exhibition: Adults – £5, Concessions – £2.50.
Typical opening hours: Tower and Exhibition – Monday to Friday from 9:30 to 17:00, closing an hour later on Saturday and Sunday.
Phone: 0207 798 9096
Website: www.westminstercathedral.org.uk

Westminster Cathedral is often missed by visitors to the city, as many stop at the nearby Westminster Abbey instead. The two churches are not to be confused. Even during peak summer season, this church is often very empty as far as visitors are concerned.

Westminster Cathedral is the principal Roman Catholic church in the UK and dates from 1903. Many walking past it may even assume it is a mosque due to the large tower and unusual architecture.

The tower is actually home to a viewing gallery (with lift access), and the church houses an exhibition – Treasures of Westminster Cathedral – where you can see rare collections of objects and learn about the church's construction. Both of these are paid admission. However, entry into the church to see the beautiful mosaics and marble-work is free.

Dining
The Northall (at Corinthia Hotel)
Nearest Station: Embankment
Address: 10a Northumberland Avenue, Corinthia Hotel, London, WC2N 5AE
Opening Hours: Breakfast – 6:30 to 10:30 on weekdays, 7:00 to 11:00 on weekends. Lunch – Monday to Saturday from 12:00 to 15:00, Sunday from 12:30 to 16:00. Dinner – Daily from 17:30 to 23:00.
Phone: 0207 930 8181
Website: www.corinthia.com/hotels/london/dining-and-bars/restaurants/the-northall

The Northall serves up delicious British-inspired food with incredible presentation, excellent service and a stunning setting. The restaurant has many different pricing options – from a mid-priced menu to fine dining.

Breakfast includes individual pastries at £4 each, crepes and pancakes at £12 to £14, as well as other a la carte items. A buffet priced at £34 per adult and £17 per child is also available. The Express Lunch set menu is £25 for two courses, or £29 for three. The Theatre set menu (17:30 to 19:00 and 21:30 to 23:00) is one pound cheaper than the lunch set menu, and offers great value for money. A Sunday brunch is also available. A la Carte mains are £14 to £35 all day long, with other pricier options also available.

Overall, this a dining experience to be revered with fantastic attention to detail and set menus that are very reasonably priced.

Gustoso – Ristorante & Enoteca
Nearest Station: Victoria
Address: 35 Willow Place, London, SW1P 1JH
Opening Hours: Restaurant – Monday to Thursday from 12:00 to 22:30, Friday & Saturday from 12:00 to 23:00, Sunday from 12:30 to 21:30. Bar – Monday to Friday from 12:00 to 22:30, Saturday from 18:00 to 22:30. The bar is closed on Sunday.
Phone: 0207 834 5778
Website: www.ristorantegustoso.co.uk

When looking for Italian in the Victoria and Westminster area, this is our number one spot. Gustoso provides delicious food at decent prices, and with good service. Portions are not huge, but adequate, and certainly not miniscule as at some higher end locations.

Prices are fair with pasta mains priced at £9 to £14, and meat or fish-based main courses priced at £10 to £17.50. Sides are £4. Specials are also available for a rotating set of dishes each and every day. Reservations are accepted and highly recommended.

Brutti & Boni – Bottega Contemporanea
Nearest Stations: Gloucester Road and High Street Kensington
Address: 14 Gloucester Road, London, SW7 4RB
Opening Hours: Monday to Wednesday from 7:00 to 19:00, with a late closing at 21:00 on Thursday and Friday. Saturday from 9:00 to 21:00, and Sunday from 10:00 to 17:00.
Phone: 0207 589 2260
Website: www.bruttiandboni.com

This place is more of a café than a restaurant, and serves tasty and authentic Italian food. With only four tables inside, and a couple outside during warmer weather, it is the perfect place to stop for a quick lunchtime snack, or something that will fill you up a bit more.

Pasta dishes are £7 to £8, delicious tortellini is £10, with focaccia and pizza slices priced at £4 to £6. Overall, prices are affordable and quality is decent.

The Lord Moon of the Mall
Nearest Station: Charing Cross
Address: 16 Whitehall, London SW1A 2DY
Opening Hours: Monday to Thursday from 8:00 to 23:30, with a late closing on Friday & Saturday at 0:00. Sunday from 08:00 to 23:00.
Phone: 0207 839 7701
Website: www.jdwetherspoon.com/pubs/all-pubs/england/london/the-lord-moon-of-the-mall-west-end

For good British pub classics in the heart of central London, give this place a visit. This is a Weatherspoon's pub, which is a large chain, but we feel it provides decent quality for the price paid in such a prime location. This is a popular establishment, though, and finding a table may be a challenge.

Breakfast meals run £2.30 to £5 including a drink, with traditional English breakfast being an option. Classic pub meals are £6.50 to £9 each, with pasta, burgers and salads being priced similarly.

Like at most pubs, the food here won't win any awards, but it is tasty and affordably price.

Accommodation
Hotel 41
Nearest Station: Victoria
Address: 41 Buckingham Palace Road, London, SW1W 0PS
Telephone: 0207 300 0041
Website: www.41hotel.com

This boutique hotel is located just steps away from Buckingham Palace with only 30 rooms and suites available. Each room is unique with a black and white theme linking them all. Service is highly personable with two members of staff for every guest and a 24-hour butler service. Rooms start at £295 per night, and suites at £599. At the time of writing, users of TripAdvisor rated this as the number one hotel in all of London.

Corinthia Hotel London
Nearest Station: Embankment and Charing Cross
Address: Whitehall Place, London, SW1A 2BD
Telephone: 0207 930 8181
Website: www.corinthia.com/hotels/london

This hotel's prime location, beautiful modern interiors and fantastic selection of restaurants make this one of the best places to stay in London. Service is exceptional as expected from a five-star establishment, and the fitness suite and indoor pool are particularly impressive. Rooms start at £357 per night.

The Grosvenor Hotel
Nearest Station: Victoria
Address: 101 Buckingham Palace Road, London, SW1W 0SJ
Telephone: 0871 376 9038
Website: www.guoman.com/hotels/united_kingdom/london/the_grosvenor_hotel/index.html

On the doorstep of Victoria station, and a five-minute stroll from Buckingham Palace, The Grosvenor Hotel has become synonymous in the area with quality. This 4-star accommodation can offer reasonable prices at times, especially considering the attention to detail here and the location. Something to be aware of is that this hotel is right next to busy Victoria Station so you may hear tannoy announcements in certain rooms if the windows are open. Rooms are available for £120 per night.

The Southbank

The Southbank area that we are describing here is actually quite a small strip of land on the south side of the river Thames, opposite Westminster and Embankment.

This is another area that is very popular with visitors, especially since the year 2000 when the London Eye opened up. Merlin Entertainments, the operator of the London Eye, has capitalized on its success by opening several attractions around The Eye.

We have also included The Imperial War Museum in this area, although it is a 10 to 15-minute walk away.

Top Tip: The London Eye, London Dungeon, London Aquarium, Shrek's Adventure and Madame Tussauds are all attractions operated by Merlin Entertainments. All of these, except Madame Tussauds, are located in the same building on the South Bank. Visit the ticket desk at any of these, or online, and consider the multi-attraction tickets on sale here. These can make for considerable savings.

Attractions

London Aquarium
Nearest Station: Waterloo
Address: County Hall, Westminster Bridge Road, Waterloo, London SE1 7PB
Entry price: Adults – £24.50, Children (3 to 15) – £18.10, Family – £82.
Typical opening hours: Open daily from 10:00 to 19:00. Last admission: one hour before closing.
Phone: 0871 663 1678
Website: www.visitsealife.com/london

Located on the South Bank, near the London Dungeon and the London Eye, this is London's largest aquarium. Inside you can see sharks, touch rays, marvel at the seahorses, delight at the penguins and much more. Learn about fish from around the world, and then bring it all back home by learning about the River Thames.

Throughout the day, talks and feeding times allow you to get to know these animals a bit better. You can see feeding sessions throughout the day for the octopuses, rays, penguins, sharks, seahorses and more.

There are also several VIP experiences available at an extra charge, including: a behind the scenes tour, turtle feeding, shark feeding, snorkeling with sharks, and marine biologist for a day.

A typical visit of the attraction will take about two hours, plus any time you take to attend optional talks and feedings.

London Eye

Nearest Station: Waterloo
Address: London Eye, Westminster Bridge Road, Waterloo, London SE1 7PB
Entry price: Adult – £23.50, Child (4 to 15) – £17.50 and Senior – £21
Typical opening hours: Open daily from 10:00 to 20:30 year round, with late closings from 21:30 to 23:30 during peak periods.
Phone: 0333 321 2001
Website: www.londoneye.com

For a unique view of London, step into one of the magnificent viewing capsules on the 135-metre (443 feet) tall London Eye. It is the world's tallest cantilevered Ferris wheel and from the top, you can see up to 40km on a clear day.

The London Eye's 32 capsules are constantly rotating, meaning a journey onboard takes 30 minutes – this the perfect speed as it doesn't feel like you are moving as you go around steadily, yet gives you enough time to get all the photos you want.

On board you can gaze across London, have a quick break on the seats in the middle of the capsules, or use one of the onboard tablets to learn about the monuments around you.

As a crowd management measure, tickets bought for the London Eye are allocated 30-minute slots. You must visit during this slot to ensure you can ride. Fast Track tickets are also available for those in a rush.

The London Eye experience can also be personalised to something even more special with the option of a private capsule for a couple, or your group; a champagne experience is also available; as well as other options.

Originally, the London Eye was known as the Millennium Wheel and was only intend to be in place for the year 2000. It is now one of the most popular attractions in the UK.

Note: Every year in January, the London Eye shuts for its annual maintenance. This usually takes place during the second and third weeks of the month. The London Eye also closes early on December 31st as London's main fireworks display is held on the London Eye itself, as well as barges on the river.

Shrek's Adventure
Nearest Station: Waterloo
Address: County Hall, Westminster Bridge Road, Waterloo, London SE1 7PB
Entry price: Adults (16+) – £27, Children – £21.85, Family – £97.70
Typical opening hours: Sunday to Friday from 10:00 to 17:00, Saturday from 10:00 to 18:00
Phone: 0871 221 2837
Website: www.shreksadventure.com

This is a new attraction to London, having only opened in July 2015, and provides some child-minded fun in the heart of town. The attraction is targeted at kids ages 6 to 12 and takes you on a journey through Shrek's world.

The entire experience lasts about 75 minutes and uses a similar format to the London Dungeon whereby guests are put into groups of about 20 and go from scene to scene immersed in Shrek's world. Along the way, guests can expect to meet Shrek and his friends, go on a crazy 4D bus ride, get lost in a mirror maze and much more in this interactive experience.

Tickets to this attraction are timed and it is possible that they sell out during busier periods of the year.

London Dungeon

Nearest Station: Waterloo
Address: County Hall, Westminster Bridge Road, Waterloo, London, SE1 7PB
Entry price: Adult – £25.95, Child (4 to 15) – £20.95 (emailed LD for prices)
Typical opening hours: Term time hours are 10:00 to 17:00 on Mon, Tues, Wed, Fri; 11:00 to 17:00 on Thurs, and 10:00 to 18:00 on weekends. Hours are extended during the school holidays.
Phone: 0871 423 2240
Website: www.thedungeons.com/london/en/

The London Dungeon has been a staple of the city since 1974, and moved to its County Hall site from Tooley Street in 2012.

With its relocation, came the addition of new scenes, the removal of others and the reconfiguration of others still. Throughout the adventure you will take a boat ride for traitors, 'drop in' on some hangings, experience Sweeney Todd's barber shop, learn all about Guy Fawkes, feel what its like to visit a Plague Doctor, encounter Jack the Ripper, and much, much more. A Victorian Tavern at the end allows you to choose your own adventure, and enjoy a complimentary drink too!

Inside, guests are put into groups of about 20 people at a time and are taken from scene to scene. Each scene depicts a period or event from London's gruesome past and uses audience interaction to bring it to life. As well the scenes with actors, there are also a couple of rides interspersed during the experience. Special physical effects throughout the attraction add to the fun.

The full experience lasts approximately 110 minutes and is not recommended for the squeamish – it is *not* a 'jump out' horror-maze type attraction, and you will learn quite a bit, but wimps should beware. Teenagers and young adults in particular are the biggest fans of this attraction.

This attraction operates on a time-slot ticketed system, if tickets are pre-booked. On the door tickets are more expensive and will require you to enter a queue, which can be an hour or more during peak times. Fast track and VIP tickets are also available.

Imperial War Museum

Nearest Stations: Lambeth North and Elephant & Castle
Address: Imperial War Museum, Lambeth Road, London, SE1 6HZ
Entry price: Free
Typical opening hours: Daily from 10:00 to 18:00
Phone: 0207 416 5000
Website: www.iwm.org.uk/visits/iwm-london

The Imperial War Museum is a fascinating collection of artifacts focusing on WWII in particular. The museum is made up of several permanent collections, including the build up to the war, the war itself, post-war life, and more.

There is also a permanent collection featuring families during WWII, the story of the First World War, a Holocaust Exhibition, and a 'Curiosities of War' section, which contains some unusual objects.

This museum is absolutely worth exploring, and regularly holds temporary exhibitions which are also free.

Dining
Locale – County Hall
Nearest Station: Waterloo
Address: County Hall, 3b Belvedere Road, London, SE1 7EP
Opening Hours: Sunday to Thursday from 12:00 to 22:30, with a late closing at 23:00 on Friday and Saturday.
Phone: 0207 401 6734
Website: www.localerestaurants.com/southbank.php

Serving delicious Italian food by the Southbank, Locale is one of our favourite places to eat in an area that is filled with other overpriced options. Here the food is tasty, plentiful and the service is good too.

Pasta and Risotta is priced at £9 to £14, with meat and fish dishes at £15 to £23, pizzas are all around the £10 mark, and salads are £8 to £10. The calzones in particular are amazing. This location also has a cocktail bar. Locale's other restaurants are in Fulham and Blackheath.

Skylon
Nearest Stations: Waterloo and Embankment
Address: Southbank Centre, Belvedere Road, Royal Festival Hall, London, SE1 8XX
Opening Hours: Restaurant hours: Lunch – Monday to Saturday from 12:00 to 14:30, Sunday from 12:00 to 15:30. Dinner – Monday to Saturday from 17:30 to 22:30. No dinner service on Sundays, but the grill and bar are open. Bar and grill times vary.
Phone: 0207 654 7800
Website: www.skylon-restaurant.co.uk

If you are after a stunning setting, a beautiful view of the River Thames and delicious food, Skylon may just be the best place on the Southbank. Staff are attentive and the location also includes a full-service bar, and a grill.

This location is a premium experience and prices reflect that, unless you opt for a set menu. A la Carte mains are priced between £24 and £39. A 6-course tasting menu is available for £59 (plus £49 for wine pairings). The set menu for lunch and dinner is £25 for two courses, and £30 for three.

The atmosphere is significantly enhanced if you can secure yourself a table overlooking the river. Reservations are accepted and recommended.

Brasserie Joel

Nearest Station: Waterloo
Address: First Floor, Park Plaza Westminster Bridge, London, SE1 7UT
Opening Hours: Lunch – Monday to Friday from 12:00 to 14:00. No lunch service on Saturday. Sunday from 12:30 to 15:30. Dinner – Monday to Saturday from 17:30 to 22:30. Sunday from 17:30 to 21:30.
Phone: 0207 620 7272
Website: www.brasseriejoel.co.uk

Located inside the Park Plaza Hotel, Brasserie Joel serves authentic French dishes, and has won numerous awards over the years.

The setting is stunning, presentation is beautiful, and service is among the best we have received for a restaurant in this price range. Mains are priced at £14.50 to £32.50. Great value set menus at lunch cost £13.95 for two courses and £15.95 for three courses, and at dinner £16.95 and £19.95 respectively. The dinner set menu is only served until 19:00.

Reservations are accepted and recommended.

Troia

Nearest Station: Waterloo
Address: 3f Belvedere Road, County Hall, London, SE1 7GQ
Opening Hours: Monday to Saturday from 12:00 to 23:30, Sunday from 12:00 to 22:30.
Phone: 0207 633 9309
Website: www.troia-restaurant.co.uk

For great quality Turkish by the Southbank, Troia is our top choice. This place has more of a café/bistro feel than a posh dining location, meaning it is more of a relaxed atmosphere. Mains are priced between £10 to £15 with grilled Turkish items, as well as staples such as steaks, pasta, salads and seafood.

Accommodation

Park Plaza Westminster Bridge

Nearest Station: Waterloo, and Westminster
Address: 200 Westminster Bridge Road, London, SE1 7UT
Telephone: 0844 415 6790
Website: www.parkplaza.co.uk/london-hotel-gb-se1-7ut/gbwestmi

This 4-star hotel is in a fantastic location on the Southbank. A short five-minute stroll will take you to Big Ben and the Houses of Parliament; the London Eye, London Dungeon and other attractions are even closer. Westminster Abbey is less than a ten-minute walk. We are fans of the modern interiors of the rooms here; the selection of dining is equally good. This is a rather large hotel with 1019 rooms. Rooms start at £161 per night.

Premier Inn London County Hall
Nearest Station: Waterloo and Westminster
Address: County Hall, Belvedere Road, Westminster, SE1 7PB
Telephone: 0871 527 8648
Website: www.premierinn.com/gb/en/hotels/england/greater-london/london/london-county-hall.html

Premier Inn is one of the chains of hotels in the UK that generally provides very good value for money, in good locations and with decent accommodation. This 3-star hotel is no except to that. The location is fantastic, being inside the same building at the London Dungeon, London Aquarium and Shrek's Adventure, and popping round the corner will take you to the London Eye and Big Ben. The location is fantastic; rooms are of good quality but are by no means luxurious. If you want a well-priced base for your stay this is a good bet. Note that there is no air conditioning at this hotel. Rooms start at £79 a night.

London Marriott Hotel County Hall
Nearest Station: Waterloo and Westminster
Address: London County Hall, Westminster Bridge Road, London, SE1 7PB
Telephone: 020 7928 5200
Website: www.marriott.co.uk/hotels/travel/lonch/

Like the Premier Inn, this is located in County Hall itself. Unlike the Premier Inn, this is a 5-star establishment. Some rooms provide views of the London Eye or Big Ben, and the location cannot be beaten. Amenities include a pool and a fitness centre, and rooms are air conditioned. Dining options include a steakhouse and bar, a lounge with afternoon tea, and an outside terrace location. Rooms start at £242 per night.

West End and Trafalgar Square

The West End is the heart of London's nightlife scene, with bars, clubs and pubs abound in this area. Soho, in particular, is the bohemian district of London. That is not to say that this is a seedy area, or unsafe, by any stretch of the imagination.

On the contrary, the West End is home to over 55 theatres (more that anywhere else in the world) and provides a huge array of dining experiences. Leicester Square in the heart of the area is also where red-carpet film premieres happen, and Chinatown is also in this area.

Mayfair is also located nearby, the home of multi-millionaires and billionaires, with house prices regularly topping £40 million. Take a stroll through Mayfair and see the beautiful buildings, with luxury shopping in New Bond Street and Old Bond Street, the beautiful area of Shepherd's Market, and Mount Street with luxury boutiques. More affordable high-street style shopping can be found on Regent Street and Oxford Street.

For cultural delights, head to Trafalgar Square and take in the National Gallery and National Portrait Gallery – both of which are free.

As you can see, there is a good chance you will be spending quite a while in this area of London.

Attractions
Royal Academy of Arts
Nearest Stations: Green Park and Piccadilly
Address: Burlington House, Piccadilly, London, W1J 0BD
Entry price: Varies by exhibition.
Typical opening hours: Saturday to Thursday from 10:00 to 18:00, with a late closing on Fridays at 22:00. Last admission: 30 minutes before closing.
Phone: 0207 300 8090
Website: www.royalacademy.org.uk

The Royal Academy of Arts holds a unique position in that it does not really house a permanent collection, and therefore has a constantly changing set of exhibitions. These exhibitions all require paid entry but the Royal Academy prides itself on providing some of the most interesting and rare exhibitions anywhere in the world, so the cost of admission is usual well worth it.

Talks are also regularly held at the Royal Academy and the vast majority of these are free; there are often other special events too. The Royal Academy also regularly runs one-hour tours covering the art, architecture and history of the building. Check the website for the exact timings of the tours – the tours are free, but donations are welcome.

Ripley's Believe it or Not! London

Nearest Station: Piccadilly
Address: The London Pavillion, 1 Piccadilly Circus, London, W1J 0DA
Entry price: Adults – £26.95, Children (4 to 15) – £19.95, Family – £79.95
Typical opening hours: 10:00 to 00:00. Last entry at 22:30. Open 365 days a year (including Christmas Day).
Phone: 0203 238 0022
Website: www.ripleyslondon.com

Ripley's prides itself on being unlike anywhere else, and its London location is no exception. It is a museum of the weird and wonderful, including historical artefacts, arts and interactive experiences. To give you an example of what you will find inside: there is a Mini Cooper covered in crystals, shrunken heads, a knitted Ferrari and much more. Tickets also include entry to a short laser game and mirror maze as part of the experience.

To honest, we are not huge fans of this attraction but others may enjoy it. If you want something unusual to add to your visit, this might be perfect for you, if you are looking for something cultural, then this is definitely not it.

Trafalgar Square

Nearest Stations: Charing Cross and Piccadilly Circus
Address: Trafalgar Square, Westminster, London, WC2N 5DN
Typical opening hours: 24/7 – Public area

Trafalgar Square is a magnificent space that celebrates Lord Admiral Horatio Nelson's victory in 1805 against the French and Spanish forces at Cape Trafalgar. Nelson's Column dominates the square, standing at 135 feet tall – the same height as his ship (the HMS Victory). Atop of the column is an 18-foot statue of Nelson himself.

The square is recognised by visitors from across the globe, and it was even used as inspiration in George Orwell's 1984 where it is referred to as Victory Square.

The famous fountains on the square date from the 1930s and were designed by Sir Edwin Lutyens. The lions around the base of Nelson's column date from the 1860s and were designed by Edwin Landseer.

Statues adorn the corners of the square: George IV (also known as the Prince Regent), Sir Charles James Napier (the British Commander-in-Chief in India in the 1840s), and Sir Henry Havelock (a British general). The fourth corner houses the fourth plinth which remained empty until 1999. Since 2005, a different sculpture has been placed on the plinth every year or two.

As of early 2016, the sculpture on the fourth plinth is "Gift Horse" by Hans Haacke which is a horse skeleton representing money, power and history. It even has a ribbon that displays the London Stock Exchange ticker. Later in 2016, "Gift Horse" is set to be replaced by "Really Good" by David Shringley, a giant hand making a thumbs-up sign with the thumb rising to 10 metres in height.

Notable buildings around Trafalgar Square include:
* The Canadian, South African, and Ugandan High Commissions
* St. Martin in the Fields Church, located to the right of The National Gallery is the church where royal births are registered. It is famous for its Crypt Café which serves warm food at pub-friendly prices in a beautiful underground setting.
* The National Gallery and The National Portrait gallery, which are covered over the following pages.

National Gallery

Nearest Stations: Charing Cross and Piccadilly Circus
Address: The National Gallery, Trafalgar Square, London WC2N 5DN
Entry price: Free
Typical opening hours: 10:00 to 18:00 (daily) and 10:00 to 21:00 (Fridays). Closed 1st January and 24th to 26th December.
Phone: 0207 747 2885
Website: www.nationalgallery.org.uk

The National Gallery is one of our favourite museums in London and, like many, is free admission. It houses some priceless works of art including notably Van Gogh's "Sunflowers", Monet's "Water Lilies" and Seurat's "Bathers at Aspires" amongst many others. The paintings on offer cover several centuries; the building's interior architecture is worth visiting for alone.

The paid-for audio guides are thoroughly recommended at £4 per adult and £3.50 for concessions. Several different audio tours are available. The National Gallery website also has suggested walking tours that you can print out or take with you on a smartphone or tablet.

The National Gallery also has a paid-for 'Sainsbury Wing', which features temporary exhibitions and collections.

National Portrait Gallery

Nearest Stations: Charing Cross, Leicester Square and Piccadilly Circus
Address: St. Martin's Place, London, WC2H 0HE
Entry price: Free
Typical opening hours: 10:00 to 18:00 (daily) and 10:00 to 21:00 (Fridays)
Phone: 0207 306 0055
Website: www.npg.org.uk

Located just off Trafalgar Square and right next door to The National Gallery, many visitors prefer this museum to its neighbour. Here, through a collection of over 200,000 portraits you can explore royalty, as well as seeing more contemporary paintings and even photographs of famous faces.

The museum is certainly worth a visit if you are in the area, and it will take a lot less time to tour than The National Gallery. Many free and paid-for temporary exhibitions are also available.

Piccadilly Circus

Nearest Station: Piccadilly Circus
Address: Piccadilly Circus, London, W1D 7ET
Typical opening hours: 24/7 – Public area

Piccadilly Circus anchors one side of the West End with the famous Piccadilly Lights, the giant advertising billboards. The first sign was put up back in 1908, and it was the world's first set of outdoor electric lights. They have been upgraded over the years and are now only on one corner of the Circus area.

Piccadilly Circus is well known for the angel-like Statue of Anteros, atop the Shaftesbury Memorial Fountain. This is dedicated to the 7th Earl of Shaftesbury who fought to stop children becoming chimney sweeps. Anteros is The Angel of Christian Charity, but he is often mistaken for Eros – the Greek god of love.

The Criterion Theatre is also located in this area – Theatreland's only underground performance space; Lillywhites next door is known as a premium sports retailer with attractive prices.

Leicester Square
Nearest Station: Leicester Square
Address: Leicester Square, London, W1D 6AP
Typical opening hours: 24/7 – Public area

Leicester Square in many ways is the heart of the West End. It is where film premieres take place for major British and international films, including James Bond, Harry Potter and Star Wars. The square is home to numerous places to eat and you can enjoy the multitude of souvenir shops available here too.

Theatre fans should visit TKTS – The Official London Theatre Ticket Booth. It sells same-day half price and discounted theatre tickets for many London shows, as well as full-priced tickets for many other shows. You can often check online in advance for what tickets they have on sale that day, and the next couple of days. The booth is open from 10:00 to 19:00 Monday to Saturday, and 11:00 to 16:30 on Sunday.

Chinatown

Nearest Stations: Piccadilly Circus and Leicester Square
Address: Gerrard St, London, W1D 6JS
Typical opening hours: 24/7 – Public area

Every major city has a Chinatown and London's is located just two minutes' walk away from the hustle and bustle of Piccadilly Circus. As soon as you enter Chinatown, you are likely to encounter one of two situations – either a very peaceful space, or a busy atmosphere. As far as food is concerned, there is something for everyone and for every price range. Many places here are cash only so be sure to ask before sitting down to eat in a restaurant, or grabbing items in a shop.

This is a small Chinatown unlike some other cities and, although it is cute, we wouldn't go out of our way to go here deliberately unless you fancy a bit of Chinese food.

Covent Garden

Nearest Station: Covent Garden
Address: Covent Garden Piazza, London, WC2E 7BB
Typical opening hours: 24/7 – Public area
Website: www.coventgarden.london

Once the place where nuns had a convent garden, this location is now a beautiful pedestrianised square surrounded by street performers, cafes, restaurants, markets, shops and even the London Transport Museum.

Make sure to explore the covered area in the middle of the square and use the steps to go into the underground portion where there are beautiful little shops to explore.

There is more on Covent Garden later in the shopping section of this guide.

London Film Museum

Nearest Station: Covent Garden
Address: 45 Wellington Street, Covent Garden, London, WC2E 7BN
Entry price: Adults – £14.50, Children (5 to 15) and Concessions – £9.50, Family – £38
Typical opening hours: 10:00 to 18:00 from Sundays to Fridays, and 10:00 to 19:00 on Saturdays
Phone: 0207 836 4913
Website: www.londonfilmmuseum.com

This is a relatively new museum, having only opened in 2008, and contains temporary exhibitions.

After the success of a Star Wars exhibit, Bond in Motion is now at the museum – this is the largest official collection of original Bond vehicles ever in London. From the vehicles themselves to concept art, and the unique inventions that make Bond the man he is, there is much to see. There is no set end date for this exhibition at the time of writing; we expect it to run until at least the end of 2016.

London Transport Museum

Nearest Station: Covent Garden
Address: Covent Garden Piazza, London, WC2E 7BB
Entry price: Adults – £17, Concessions – £14.50.
Typical opening hours: From 10:00 to 18:00 on Monday to Thursday and weekends, and 11:00 to 18:00 on Friday. Last admission is at 17:15.
Phone: 0207 379 6344
Website: www.ltmuseum.co.uk

The London Transport Museum is situated in the heart of Covent Garden. It explains and conserves the heritage of London's transportation, telling its story over the last 200 years. You can learn about how London's basic transport system functioned in the past, the arrival of the world's first underground railway, and how transport is intricately linked with London's transformation and expansion.

This is one of our favourite museums in London and it is truly fascinating seeing how important transportation has been to London's evolution. The London Transport Museum is enjoyable for visitors of all ages with many interactive exhibitions, as well as actual buses and underground trains dating back over 100 years.

Individual tickets purchased for the museum are valid for unlimited visits for the named person during one year.

Somerset House & The Courtauld Gallery

Nearest Stations: Temple and Covent Garden
Address: Somerset House, Strand, London, WC2R 1LA
Entry price: Somerset House is open access. Exhibitions in the Embankment galleries are £12.50 for adults and £9.50 for concessions. Courtauld Gallery tickets are £7 for adults, £6 for concessions and free for under 18s.
Typical opening hours: Embankment Galleries and Courtauld Gallery from 10:00 to 18:00 daily, Fountain Court and other public areas from 07:30 or 08:00 to 23:00
Phone: 0207 848 2777 for the Courtauld Gallery and 0207 845 4600 for Somerset House
Website: www.somersethouse.org.uk and www.courtauld.ac.uk

Somerset House is a cultural centre hosting several artistic events. The centre courtyard of the building is home to an ice rink in the winter, and dancing fountains in the summer.

There is also the Embankment Gallery area which contains temporary exhibitions; the Courtauld Gallery is home to French impressionist paintings. Public areas of the building are free to explore, but the galleries are paid admission.

Free guided tours of the building are offered on select days of the week. Check the website for exact dates and timing.

Royal Courts of Justice

Nearest Stations: Temple, Holborn and Chancery Lane
Address: Strand, London, WC2A 2LL
Phone: 0207 947 6000 (07789 751248 for the tours)
Website: www.justice.gov.uk/courts/rcj-rolls-building

Dating from 1882, this stunning building is home to the High Court and Court of Appeal of England and Wales.

Members of the public can go inside and sit in the public gallery to hear court in session, apart from certain private matters. There is no charge to do this.

In addition, the RCJ runs very under-publicised tours of the building delving into its architecture, art and the history of the building. Tours run for about two hours and are priced at £12 per adult, £10 for concessions, and £5 per child (under 14). Tours can be booked by calling 07789 751248 or via email at **rcjtours@talktalk.net**. These tours run regularly, subject to there being enough interest.

Benjamin Franklin House
Nearest Stations: Charing Cross and Embankment
Address: 36 Craven Street, London, WC2N 5NF
Entry price: Historical Experience: Adults – £7, Children (Under 16) – Free. Architectural Tours: Adults – £3.50, Children (Under 16) – Free.
Typical opening hours: Set show and tour times from 12:00 to 16:15. Box office opens at 10:30.
Phone: 0207 839 2006
Website: www.benjaminfranklinhouse.org

Come and visit the only surviving home of the US Founding Father, where Benjamin Franklin spent sixteen years living and working on the eve of the American Revolution.

The house dates from the 1730s and still has many of the original features intact, including the central staircase and the windows.

There are 25-minute architectural tours of the location, as well as a 45-minute "historical experience", which combines learning with theatre.

Cleopatra's Needle

Nearest Station: Embankment
Address: Victoria Embankment, London, WC2N 6
Entry price: Free
Typical opening hours: 24/7 – Public area

Cleopatra's Needle is one of the most fascinating historical artifacts in the whole city and is one of the oldest things displayed outdoors publicly – it is between 3000 and 3500 years old. The Needle is situated on the Victoria Embankment, a short troll from Embankment station.

Cleopatra's Needle is an ancient Egyptian obelisk presented to the UK by Egyptian ruler Muhammad Ali to commemorate the victory at the Battle of the Nile in 1819. The Needle has two "twins" in Paris and New York City.

Fun Fact: Curiously, the sphinxes at the base of the obelisk were placed incorrectly and instead of looking outwards to "guard" the needle, they are just staring at it instead.

Handel House Museum & Jimi Hendrix Flat

Nearest Stations: Bond Street and Oxford Circus
Address: 25 Brook Street, Mayfair, London, W1K 4HB
Entry price: Adults – £7.50 to either the museum of the flat, £10 for both. Children – £3 to either the museum of the flat, £5 for both.
Typical opening hours: 10:00 to 18:00 on Tuesday, Wednesday, Friday and Saturday; 10:00 to 20:00 on Thursday; and 12:00 noon to 18:00 on Sunday. Closed Monday. Last admission is 30 minutes before closing.
Phone: 0207 495 1685
Website: www.handelhendrix.org

These two visitor locations are located right next door to each other on Brook Street. Number 25 was previously home to Handel who lived and composed there for 36 years to 1759, and the top floor of the house next door was Jimi Hendrix's flat in 1968 and 1969.

At the Handel House Museum, you can see four restored rooms, as well as temporary exhibitions about the man himself. The main living area of Hendrix's flat has also been restored, and a permanent exhibition about Hendrix is also in place.

You can buy separate tickets for each location, or joint tickets for both are available, which will save you money.

Dining

The West End area of London has a fantastic variety of culinary delights from Italian to Chinese, Japanese to British, and American to Indian.

Being the West End, this area is filled with both Londoners and visitors to the city, meaning that there are many places in the area that we would consider 'tourist traps' with high prices and sub-par food, so check restaurant review websites before choosing where to eat.

Having said that, the West End does contain some of the best places to eat in the whole city too, so it is well worth considering eating here. There are buffets, table-service and fast food places in every direction you look, and prices on the whole are competitive as restaurants want to attract theatre-goers and evening crowds.

Hawksmoor – Air Street
Nearest Station: Piccadilly Circus
Address: 5a Air Street, London, W1J 0AD, England
Opening hours: Lunch – Monday to Friday from 12:00 to 15:00. Dinner – Monday to Thursday from 17:00 to 22:30, and Fridays from 17:00 to 23:00. Saturday – Open all day from 12:00 to 23:00. Sunday – Open all day from 12:00 to 22:30.
Phone: 0207 406 3980
Website: www.thehawksmoor.com/locations/airstreet/

This upscale Seafood and Steak restaurant has become very 'on trend' over the last few years. They serve some of the best cuts of steak we have ever eaten. Perhaps surprisingly for a place that serves steaks, the seafood here is delicious too.

Pricing is on the slightly higher end but this is meant to be a slightly upscale experience. Seafood is priced at £20 to £48 for a whole fish, with Turbot priced at £13 per 100g, and the delicious Dartmouth Lobster at £5 per 100g. Steaks can either be bought pre-cut for between £18.50 and £35, and vary in size from 300g to 400g. Large cuts are priced at £8.25 to £13 per 100g, and start at 500g in size.

A Sunday roast option is available for £20. We find the express menu to be a particularly good deal at £25 for two courses, and £28 for three. It is available Monday to Saturday all day except 18:30 to 22:00.

This particular location is just seconds from Piccadilly Circus. Other Hawksmoor London locations include: Seven Dials (round the corner in Covent Garden), Guildhall and Spitalfields (in The City), and Knightsbridge. Reservations are accepted.

Quattro Passi
Nearest Station: Green Park
Address: 34 Dover Street, London, W1S 4NG
Opening Hours: Open daily from 12:00 to 15:00, and 18:30 to 22:30 (last orders). Closed on Sundays.
Phone: 0203 096 1444
Website: www.quattropassi.co.uk

This upscale Italian restaurant boasts lavish interiors, a signature menu and a Michelin-Starred Head Chef, Antonio Mellino.

Appetizers/antipasti range from £12 to £20. Pasta dishes are £16 to £22, and other mains such as fish and meat are £25 to £35. A "business lunch" offer is available Monday to Friday from 12:00 to 15:00, with two courses priced at £26, and three courses at £34. Prices are on the higher side but we feel the experience, service and taste merit this. Reservations are accepted and recommended.

Misato
Nearest Stations: Piccadilly Circus and Leicester Square
Address: 11 Wardour Street, London, W1D 6PG
Opening hours: Daily from 12:00 to 23:00
Phone: 0207 734 0808

Japanese food just steps away from Chinatown? That's right! Misato is one of the most affordable quality meals in central London in our opinion. With 8-piece mixed sashimi sets at £7.50, sushi pieces are £1 each, and maki costs even less; you can have a decent meal here for under £15 per person. Bento boxes are £8.50, and they also serve light meals and rice dishes at £5 to £8 a pop. Even the beers are under £3. With good quality food, and large portions, at an affordable price, Misato is great spot to dine at.

There may be waits at peak periods as this is a popular place and is quite small. Misato does not currently have its own dedicated website, and does not accept reservations.

Yauatcha
Nearest Stations: Piccadilly Circus, Leicester Square, Oxford Circus and Tottenham Court Road
Address: 15-17 Broadwick Street, London, W1F 0DL
Opening hours: Daily from 12:00 to 22:00, with a late closing at 22:30 on Friday and Saturday.
Phone: 020 7494 8888
Website: www.yauatcha.com

Serving some of the best contemporary Cantonese food in London, and located outside the Chinatown area, Yauatcha offers upscale dining. A la Carte prices vary wildly, from the £9.20 egg fried rice to the £38 Lobster vermicelli pot. Lunch and dinner "signature" menus are also available for £40 and £45 per person respectively, with a minimum of two people dining.

The service is attentive and the interior is simple but elegant. The cake selection is to die for. Reservations are accepted and recommended.

Savoir Faire
Nearest Stations: Tottenham Court Road and Holborn
Address: 42 New Oxford Street, London, WC1A 1EP
Opening Hours: Daily from 12:00 to 22:30
Phone: 0207 436 0707
Website: www.savoir.co.uk

With London's French population booming and standing at over 66,000 and counting, it's no surprise to find quality French fare in the city. Savoir Faire is located on the edge of the West End, less than a 2-minute walk from The British Museum.

Unique to Savoir Faire is the fact that everything is prepared fresh on the premises – from the mains, to the bread, the sauces and even the dessert.

A two-course set lunch menu is priced at £14.90. The a la carte lunch menu includes salads, burgers, omelets and sandwiches – all priced at £5 to £10. Muscles, beef and lamb are priced between £7 and £18.

A two-course dinner menu is also available for £23.90, with a vegetarian menu available at £14.90. Main courses such as Rib Eye Steak, Fillet of Sea Bass and Duck Margaret are all £18 a la Carte at dinner.

All meals include a basket of fresh bread, as is customary in France, and in our opinion the food is very affordably priced and of excellent quality. Reservations are accepted.

Accommodation
The Ritz
Nearest Station: Green Park
Address: 150 Piccadilly, London, W1J 9BR
Telephone: 0207 493 8181
Website: www.theritzlondon.com

Founded by César Ritz in 1906, this 5-star hotel was intended to be the best in London, and in many ways it has become that. It is one of London's most well-known hotels, and the one that people usually refer to when speaking of quality.

Despite the large facades, there are only 111 rooms and 23 suites at The Ritz, so it always retains a feel of exclusivity. The smallest rooms are 215 square feet (20 square metres) in size.

The interiors are palatial and its easy to understand why The Royal Family has held several events here over the years; The Ritz was also The Queen Mother's favourite place to go to for afternoon tea.

With the casino in the basement, and the renowned afternoon tea location, there is always something to do here. The service is, of course, unrivalled. Rooms at The Ritz start at £396 per night.

The Savoy Hotel
Nearest Station: Charing Cross, Embankment and Temple
Address: Strand, London WC2R 0EU
Telephone: 0207 836 4343
Website: www.fairmont.com/savoy-london

This 5-star hotel is another of the most famous hotels in central London, and it is very well located indeed. Within a radius of a 15-minute walk you can visit the Southbank for the London Eye, Big Ben, Trafalgar Square, and all of the West End. The rooms all offer excellent views.

The hotel led to some key innovations in the hotel trade, being the first to be lit by electric lamps, have electric lifts, and en-suite bathrooms in each room. Things that we take for granted nowadays!

The hotel has 4 restaurants, 2 bars, a spa and pool, and a health club. Rooms start at £351 per night.

Travelodge London Covent Garden
Nearest Station: Covent Garden and Temple
Address: 10 Drury Lane, High Holborn, London, WC2B 5RE
Telephone: 0871 984 6245
Website: www.travelodge.co.uk/hotels/318/London-Central-Covent-Garden-hotel

Travelodge is a budget hotel chain that offers simple, clean rooms around the UK. This location is no exception. Set in the heart of the West End, a short walk in any direction will take you to a number of attractions. Amenities are basic, limited to a bar/café, with no on-site restaurant. There are a number of Travelodge hotels in central London. Rooms at this 2-star hotel start at £49 per night.

Kensington & The Museums

Kensington is one of the most affluent area in the world, with house prices averaging in the millions; a 5-bedroom luxury flat was even recently sold for £140 million.

The area is very much residential but also offers a collection of London's finest museums. Those looking for a bit of royalty will be pleased to find both Kensington Palace in a park called Kensington Gardens, and the Royal Albert Hall, a live performance venue.

Shoppers will not be disappointed with the selection of luxury goods on offer on High Street Kensington, King's Road, and Harrods – the largest department store in Europe at over one million square feet in size.

Finally, sports fans can visit Stamford Bridge, Chelsea F.C.'s stadium.

Attractions
Natural History Museum

Nearest Station: South Kensington
Address: Cromwell Rd, London, SW7 5BD
Entry price: Free
Typical opening hours: Daily from 10:00 to 17:50. Last entry at 17:30.
Phone: 0207 942 5000
Website: www.nhm.ac.uk

The Natural History Museum has long been a popular haunt for both Londoners and tourists alike but since most museums were made free to visitors in 2001, the popularity of this museum soared.

The museum was purpose-built and opened in 1881 moving much of the collection from the British Museum here.

It is easy to see why the museum is so popular with a wide variety of permanent exhibitions in its collection. Throughout your visit you can go from marveling dinosaur skeletons and an animatronic T-Rex, to geological finds, to the enormous Mammals area, and even walk past scientists working at the museums Darwin Centre.

The museum also often offers fascinating temporary exhibitions, which are paid admission, as well as special events such as a 'Night at the Museum'-style sleepover, and after-hours' "lates" events.

Science Museum

Nearest Station: South Kensington
Address: Exhibition Road, London, SW7 2DD
Entry price: Donation based – £5 suggested
Typical opening hours: Open daily from 10:00 to 18:00. The museum closes at 19:00 during school holidays.
Phone: 0207 942 4000
Website: www.sciencemuseum.org.uk

Located right next to the Natural History Museum, the Science Museum, has also seen a surge in visitors since it became free. It is an absolutely fascinating museum and one of our favourite museums anywhere in the world.

Inside you can learn all about outer space and the moon landings, take part in interactive exhibitions, see how steam trains and airplanes have revolutionised transport and much more. A whole area dedicated to young children with shows and interactive exhibitions makes learning fun too.

Also inside the museum is an IMAX screen showing scientific movies, as well as a simulator attraction and numerous kids play areas. There are also many places to stop and eat. Temporary exhibitions and special events mean there are always a multitude of reasons to keep coming back.

On the last Wednesday of each month from 18:45 to 22:00 the museum hosts 'Lates', a free adult-only night.

During our last visit to the museum we were disappointed to see that the "free" aspect of this museum has changed. They now require you to go past a ticket desk where staff will ask you to donate to enter. It is not compulsory but it can be awkward if you were expecting open entry like other museums. The suggested £5 donation is exceptional value but we'd rather they charge properly or just make it open access with donation points on the way out like other museums.

Victoria & Albert Museum

Nearest Station: South Kensington
Address: Cromwell Road, London, SW7 2RL
Entry price: Free
Typical opening hours: Open daily from 10:00 to 17:45, with a late closing at 22:00 on Fridays.
Phone: 0207 942 2000
Website: www.vam.ac.uk

An absolute gem of a museum that shouldn't be missed. We like to think of the V&A as London's *Musée du Louvre* in terms of grandeur and variety of exhibitions. Collections include architecture, books, ceramics, fashion, furniture, painting, textiles and much more.

Many temporary exhibitions are offered throughout the year too – these require an entry fee.

It is not really a location we would take children to as there is not very much to stimulate their senses, but adults of all ages will appreciate the wonder of the V&A. The building, courtyard and exhibitions are delightful.

Kensington Palace

Nearest Stations: High Street Kensington, Notting Hill Gate and Queensway
Address: Kensington Gardens, London, W8 4PX
Entry price: Adults – £16.50, Concessions – £13.70, Children (under 16) – Free
Typical opening hours: Daily from 10:00 to 17:00 (winter). Extended hours in summer.
Phone: 0203 166 6000
Website: www.hrp.org.uk/kensington-palace/

Kensington Palace, unlike many other royal palaces, is open to the public year-round (except 24th to 26th December).

The story of the palace spans back over 400 years to 1605 when the first house was built on this site – a small two-floor building. By 1689, William III and Mary II had bought the house to convert it into a palace.

The palace was the former home of Princess Diana, and is now home to the Duke and Duchess of Cambridge (William and Kate).

During a visit to the palace you can enjoy the King's Staircase, the King and Queen's state apartments, the "Victoria Revealed" exhibition, and much more.

Royal Albert Hall Tours

Nearest Stations: South Kensington, Gloucester Road and High Street Kensington
Address: Kensington Gore, Kensington, London, SW7 2AP
Entry price: Tours: Adults – £12.75 to £15.75, Concessions – £10.75 to £13.75, Children – £5.75 to £8.75.
Typical opening hours: Tours depart regularly – generally between 10:00 and 15:00.
Phone: 0207 589 8212
Website: www.royalalberthall.com

This 140-year-old location is a music and entertainment venue, so that side of it will be covered later in this guide. However, tours of this magnificent building are also available.

Several tours are offered:
* The Grand Tour is an hour-long journey through the public areas of the Hall, including the beautiful auditorium, the breathtaking view from the Gallery and even offers exclusive access to the Royal Retiring Room. An optional afternoon tea experience can be added onto the end of this tour for an additional £16.
* The Secret History Tour is a very different kind of tour retelling the stories of "ghost hunters to gangsters, swindlers and charlatans", and much more.
* The Behind the Scenes Tour does what it says on the tin, as you visit areas not normally accessible by the public – including under the stage, inside a dressing room, and the loading bay. This tour lasts approximately one hour.

* The Inside Out Architectural Tour gives you an insight into how this building was designed both inside and out.

During the summer BBC Prom season, a "Story of the Proms" tour is also available.

Brompton Oratory

Nearest Station: South Kensington
Address: Brompton Road, London, SW7 2RP
Entry price: Free
Typical opening hours: 6:30 to 20:00
Website: www.bromptonoratory.co.uk

Also known as The Church of the Immaculate Heart of Mary, this astounding Catholic Church dates from 1884 and is worth popping your head in for a few minutes to see. It is very similar in style to classic Italian basilicas. From the stunning High Altar to St. Wilfred's Chapel, and the beautiful dome to the pulpit, there is a gem around every corner inside.

This is a real working church, and it is not at all a visitor attraction, so do bear that in mind when visiting. Feel free to attend a service if you are so inclined. It is located right next door to the the Victoria & Albert Museum.

Saatchi Gallery

Nearest Station: Sloane Square
Address: Duke of York's HQ, King's Road, London, SW3 4RY
Entry price: Free
Typical opening hours: Daily from 10:00 to 18:00. Last entry is at 17:30.
Phone: 0207 811 3070
Website: www.saatchigallery.com

The Saatchi Gallery is home to contemporary art and has a regularly rotating set of exhibitions. Curiously, a lot of the art on display here is by lesser-known, or unknown, artists who are subsequently offered the opportunity for shows worldwide – in this way, the gallery is a gem that gives back to artists as much as it inspires visitors. All exhibitions are free.

Brompton Cemetery

Nearest Stations: Earl's Court and Fulham Broadway (Underground), and West Brompton (Overground)
Address: Fulham Road, London, SW10 9UG
Entry price: Free
Typical opening hours: Opens daily at 8:00. Closing times vary seasonally from 16:00 in winter to 20:00 in summer.
Phone: 0207 352 1201
Website: www.royalparks.org.uk/parks/brompton-cemetery

Perhaps an unusual place to visit whilst on holiday in London, Brompton Cemetery has seen its popularity and visitor numbers soar in recent years – now over 700,000 people visit every year.

Brompton Cemetery is one of Britain's oldest, opened in 1840, and has over 205,000 people buried there and is still a working cemetery to this day.

Notable graves include those of Emmeline Pankhurst (one of the suffragettes), William Claude Kirby (the first chairman of Chelsea F.C.) and Henry Cole (founder of the Victoria & Albert Museum), amongst many others.

Fun Fact: It is said that Beatrix Potter was inspired by some of the names on the tombstones for her stories – there is even a Peter Rabbett buried here.

Dining
Chez Patrick
Nearest Stations: High Street Kensington and Earl's Court
Address: 7 Stratford Road, London, W8 6RF
Opening Hours: Lunch – Daily from 12:00 to 14:45. Dinner – Monday to Saturday from 18:45 to 23:00. No dinner service on Sunday.
Phone: 0207 937 6388
Website: www.chez-patrick.co.uk

This small and intimate French restaurant is a real gem in the South Kensington area. With room for only 60 people over two floors, the cozy ambiance feels very much like dining at a friend's house. The interior resembles a restaurant by the Med, and you might just forget you are in the heart of London. The food is delicious, portions are large and the service is friendly.

Ingredients arrive daily and are prepared by head chef Alain Patrat, who has over 25 years of experience in the restaurant trade.

The lunchtime set menus are particularly good value. A three course meal is £13.50 on weekdays, and £16.90 on weekends. A la Carte fish and mains are priced at £15 to £19. The wine list is French and reasonably extensive. Reservations are available.

Pizzetta Pizza
Nearest Station: South Kensington
Address: 22 Bute Street, South Kensington, London, SW7 3EX
Opening Hours: Daily from 08:00 to 23:00.
Phone: 0207 584 9090
Website: www.pizzettapizza.com

For fresh pizza in South Kensington, there is no better place to go that Pizzetta Pizza. This place is small, and informal, and serves some of the best food around.

The pizza is authentic, fresh, and the staff are fantastic. Pizza is sold by the slice, and £2.50 is the price. Pasta dishes are a mere £4.80, and soups are £2.50. The coffee is delicious too, as are the cakes.

For a fantastic deal, visit during Happy Hour on Thursdays from 17:00 to 20:00. They give you a free slice of pizza with every drink. Bargain!

Pizzetta Pizza also has another location in Victoria, with a Mayfair location coming soon. Reservations are not available for Pizzetta.

Bosphorus
Nearest Station: South Kensington
Address: 59 Old Brompton Road, South Kensington, London, SW7 3JS
Opening Hours: Daily from 11:00 to 23:30
Phone: 0207 584 4048

Walking past this may seem like your run-of-the-mill local kebab shop, but that couldn't be further from the truth. The food here is simply delicious, and prices are very affordable. Having been here for 40 years, it is a neighbourhood staple.

Authentic Turkish kebabs are served in large portions including a pitta and salad, all for £6 to £7.50. If you are a fan of chips with your kebab, however, you won't find those here. There is a small seating area where you can eat in, or you can take away.

The Muffin Man Tea Shop
Nearest Stations: Earl's Court and Gloucester Road
Address: 12 Wrights Lane, London, W8 6TA
Opening Hours: Monday to Saturday from 8:00 to 20:00, Sunday from 9:00 to 20:00
Phone: 0207 937 6652

For a great breakfast option, make Muffin Man a stop. With a full English breakfast available for £9.50, this tea shop provides value for money in the heart of Kensington.

It's not just breakfast however, as cakes, cupcakes and tea are available throughout the day, as well as salads, sandwiches, paninis and soups. Most of the items on the menu are £2 to £4, with only a few rare items over £7.

This is a great place for a quick bite and you can make your meal as small or as large as you like with all the small add-on items. Great for those days when you don't need a full lunch or dinner.

Accommodation
The Milestone
Nearest Station: High Street Kensington
Address: 1 Kensington Court, London, W8 5DL
Telephone: 020 7917 1000
Website: www.milestonehotel.com

This luxury, 5-star hotel's origins date back to 1689. As well as the classic rooms and suites, there are six self-contained apartments too. An on-site restaurant, afternoon tea experience, a conservatory area, a spa and a fitness room are just some of the on-site amenities. Rooms start at £266 per night.

EasyHotel Earl's Court
Nearest Station: Earl's Court
Address: 42-48 West Cromwell Road, London, SW5 9QL
Telephone: 0207 373 7457
Website: www.easyhotel.com/hotels/united-kingdom/london-earls-court

EasyHotel is our new favourite budget chain when needing a no-frills place to stay. From the creators of low-cost airline EasyJet, there is now an affordable and clean accommodation option in central London.

If you will just be spending a few hours in your hotel room each day, don't need the luxury facilities and want to save some money, then we highly recommend EasyHotel.

As the hotels are all brand new or have recently been refurbished, you won't find aging rooms here. When we say these hotels are no frills, that really is the case – the cheapest rooms don't even have windows and are very small; TV and Wi-Fi access are optional, and extra charges.

This particular location is close to a tube station and a 15-minute walk to Kensington's museums. Like the other EasyHotel locations, it is cheap and clean. Rooms start £29 per night. There is another EasyHotel location nearby in South Kensington.

The Villa Kensington

Nearest Station: Gloucester Road
Address: 10-11 Ashburn Gardens, London, SW7 4DG
Telephone: 0207 370 6605
Website: www.thevillakensington.co.uk

This 3-star hotel provides affordable accommodation, and is a 10-minute walk from the Kensington Museums. An onsite café-style restaurant and bar, serves a full English breakfast at a bargain £5.50 and a continental breakfast is included in most room rates.

It's an upgrade from the aforementioned EasyHotel in terms of comfort and location, but this is by no means a luxurious place to stay. The 3-star rating feels deserved in our opinion. Rooms start at £68 per night.

The City

The City of London (or just 'The City') is an area located right in the centre of London itself. Having been founded by the Romans as Londinium about 2000 years ago, The City has morphed into the financial heart of London. Very few people live here, but over half a million people call it their place of work.

Having suffered many disasters over the years, including The Great Plague and The Great Fire of London in the 17th century, The City is filled with fascinating historical sites in every direction you look, including St. Paul's Cathedral, The Monument and the Tower of London. Many museums are also dotted around this area.

Attractions
Tower of London

Nearest Stations: Tower Hill and Tower Gateway
Address: Tower of London, London, EC3N 4AB
Entry price: Adult – £24.50, Child (5 to 15) – £11, Concession – £18.70. A family ticket is priced at £60.70.
Typical opening hours: On Tuesdays to Saturdays, 09:00 to 17:30 from March to October, and 09:00 to 16:30 from November to February. The attraction opens at 10:00 on Sundays and Mondays year-round.
Phone: 0203 166 6000
Website: www.hrp.org.uk/tower-of-london/

Of all the major visitor attractions in London to visit, the Tower of London is undoubtedly our favourite. It is amazing to see this 900-year-old castle still standing in the very heart of London.

The Tower was originally constructed for William the Conqueror who invaded London in 1066. By 1078, a castle had been built for him on the edge of the City of London. At the time, the Tower of London was just the 'White Tower', which currently stands in the centre of the site. It has expanded immensely over the last 900 years.

The Tower has been home to three coronations – Edward V, Edward VIII and Lady Jane Grey and is also notorious for having been the home of Henry VIII who had six wives throughout his lifetime.

The sheer size of the Tower of London cannot be underestimated and it is possible to spend an entire day touring this attraction – we recommend a minimum of 3 to 4 hours.

Most of the Tower of London is self-guided, as you choose which areas to explore. However, we recommend you do one of the Yeoman Warder or 'Beefeater' tours to begin your day. These depart from near the entrance to the Tower and are included in the price of admission. The tour lasts approximately one hour, with tours leaving every 30 minutes (last tour 15:30 in summer, 14:30 in winter). Throughout the tour, you will get an inside look at the gruesome history of the Tower and visit some of the key locations throughout the site.

Once you have done the tour, it is time to explore the rest of the site. Every direction you go in there are intriguing exhibitions to visit, you can also walk across the top of the castle's walls, see The Queen's Crown Jewels up close, and much more.

Top Tip: If you have a chance, ask the Warders what its like to live inside the Tower – and yes, they pay rent.

Inner and Middle Temple

Nearest Station: Temple
Address: Temple, London, EC4Y 7BB
Entry price: Free

This beautiful area located just by the Victoria Embankment in the City of London is where lawyers and barristers are educated. Here, you can visit the beautiful grounds, courtyards and gardens, which are a serene oasis in the heart of the city. These usually close at sunset.

Also notable in the area is the stunning Temple Church founded by the Knight's Templar in the late 12th century – this is part of a story that was popularised in The Da Vinci Code.

The Bank of England Museum

Nearest Station: Bank
Address: Threadneedle Street, London, EC2R 8AH
Entry price: Free
Typical opening hours: Monday to Friday from 10:00 to 17:00. Last admission 30 minutes before closing. Closed on weekends.
Phone: 0207 601 5545
Website: www.bankofengland.co.uk

This museum, located inside the Bank of England itself, is filled with things to see. Learn about the 300 years of the Bank's history, pick up a gold bar, learn about how fraud is reduced through advanced security systems on bank notes, learn about how the economy works, and much more. This is a great museum for people of all ages and contains a variety of interactive exhibits.

Museum of London

Nearest Stations: St. Paul's, Barbican and Moorgate
Address: 150 London Wall, London, EC2Y 5HN
Entry price: Free
Typical opening hours: Daily from 10:00 to 18:00. Closed 24th to 26th December.
Phone: 0207 001 9844
Website: www.museumoflondon.org.uk

The Museum of London is the perfect place to get an insight into how London has evolved over the last 2000 years. Here you can see how the city has changed from a Roman settlement to a place with over 8.6 million residents. Learn about the Plague, the Great Fire of London, the Victorian expansion, and much more along the way.

This is one of our favourite museums in London and the permanent collection is fascinating. Without exception, all temporary exhibitions (paid admission) we have seen here have been of a very high quality too.

St. Paul's Cathedral

Nearest Station: St. Paul's
Address: St. Paul's Churchyard, London, EC4M 8AD
Entry price: Adults – £18, Concessions – £16, Children (6 to 17) – £8, Family – £44
Typical opening hours: Monday to Saturday from 8:30 to 16:30. No sightseeing on Sunday.
Phone: 020 7246 8350
Website: www.stpauls.co.uk

The grandest of architect Sir Christopher Wren's churches, St. Paul's Cathedral is an architectural masterpiece.

Measuring 365-feet tall and situated on the top of Ludgate Hill – the highest point in the City of London – it can be seen from much of the surrounding area.

From the top of St. Paul's, at the Golden Gallery (528 steps up), visitors can get one of our favourite views of central London – you can look west towards Westminster with the London Eye, to the north is the Barbican Centre, east reveals The City and its impressive skyscrapers, as well as Tower Bridge, whilst looking south you can see The Shard, Shakespeare's Globe Theatre and The Tate Modern.

As well as the viewing area at the Golden Gallery, the Stone Gallery further down provides a good view. Other areas of note include The Crypt, the interior dome, the Geometric Staircase and more.

Multimedia guides are included in the price of admission, and there are guided tours which depart regularly throughout the day. The most comprehensive guided tour lasts 90 minutes and enters areas not usually open to the public. You should allow 1.5 to 2 hours to see the church in its entirety, including climbing to the top.

Those wishing to worship can enter the church at no cost, but will not be able to enter the visitor galleries or climb to the top – tickets must be shown to do this.

Tower Bridge

Nearest Stations: Tower Hill, Tower Gateway and London Bridge
Address: Tower Bridge Rd, London, SE1 2UP
Entry price: No charge to cross the bridge. Exhibition charges are as follows: Adults – £9, Children (5 to 15) – £3.90, Concessions – £6.30.
Typical opening hours: The bridge itself is open 24/7. The exhibition's summer opening hours (April to September) are 10:00 – 17:30 (last admission) and the winter opening hours (October to March) are 09:30 – 17:00 (last admission). Closed 24th to 26th December.
Phone: 0207 403 3761
Website: www.towerbridge.org.uk

There are a few notable bridges on the river Thames that you may wish to explore. Tower Bridge is likely to be at the top of your list, however, as it is undoubtedly the most famous of them all and a true symbol of London.

Unfortunately, despite the bridge's popularity, it is often incorrectly called London Bridge by tourists, which is actually the next bridge down the river.

The bridge itself was only unveiled in 1894, and took eight years to construct. It was the result of a public competition and Horace Jones (who was an architect) came up with the winning design.

The design allowed foot passengers to cross at all times whilst allowing ships with large masts through. The way this worked was by the road bridge bascules lifting up, temporarily stopping traffic, to allow the ship through. Pedestrians would climb up the towers on either end, walk across the walkway at the top and come back down the other side.

Nowadays, the bridge still does lift up in this same way about three times a day, or 1000 times per year. You can check the Tower Bridge website to see opening times scheduled well into the future. Today, the process is very quick and pedestrians no longer use the walkways at the top to cross – these are now part of the Tower Bridge Exhibition. The best place to get photos of the bridge when the bascules are lifted up is from London Bridge which runs parallel, or by the walls of the Tower of London closest to the Thames.

The Tower Bridge Exhibition (paid entry) allows you access inside the towers, as well as the pedestrian walkway across the top and even the engine rooms underneath. 2014 saw the addition of a new glass floor to certain parts of the walkways meaning that, if you choose to, you can look straight down at the traffic below. This attraction is well worth a visit and covers both technological advances and the history of the bridge itself, as well as the river Thames.

Fun Fact: The stone cladding on the outside of the bridge's structure is used to make it appear older than it actually is and to enable it to blend with the Tower of London's 900-year-old walls. The structural support columns are actually made of steel.

Fleet Street

Nearest Stations: Temple and Chancery Lane
Address: Fleet Street, London, EC4A 2BH

Fleet Street is named after the River Fleet which is a major underground river in London. Up until the 1980s, the street was famous for housing the British national newspapers. Fleet Street is still a phrase used today when speaking about newspapers several years after they have left the area.

Fleet Street has quite a few notable sights. Starting in the West you can enjoy the Royal Courts of Justice (covered elsewhere in this section). Directly opposite the Courts, pop into Twinings (address: 216 Strand) – a tea merchant which has stood here for over 300 years – notice how the shops around this one now tower above it.

You can also see The Temple Bar Memorial monument here which stands proud with a dragon atop – it marks the location of Sir Christopher Wren's previous Temple Bar entrance to the city, which has now been moved next to nearby St. Paul's Cathedral.

Moving further east along Fleet Street, just a few doors down, look for a tiny alleyway called "Hen and Chicken Court", it is here The Demon Barber of Fleet Street – Sweeney Todd – used to slash the throats of his victims, according to the popular urban legend.

Fleet Street is very well known for its pubs. Our favourite, for atmosphere alone is Ye Olde Cheshire Cheese, which was rebuilt in 1667 – take the staircase downstairs and you will notice how much smaller people were back then: the headroom on the stairs is non-existant.

St. Bride's Church is another favourite spot of ours and is located just before you reach the end of Fleet Street going east. The unusual spire of this church is said to have been the inspiration for today's multi-tier wedding cake when a local baker used the spire as inspiration.

By the time you reach the end of Fleet Street you will have a stunning view of nearby St Paul's Cathedral.

Fun Fact: Dragons are the guardians of the City of London, and you will find them on the City of London logo. You will find dragon statues at most major road entrance to the City of London including Fleet Street, Victoria Embankment, London Bridge and by the Tower of London. Our favourites – and the grandest – are the Victoria Embankment duo, located just a short stroll from Temple station.

Guildhall Art Gallery

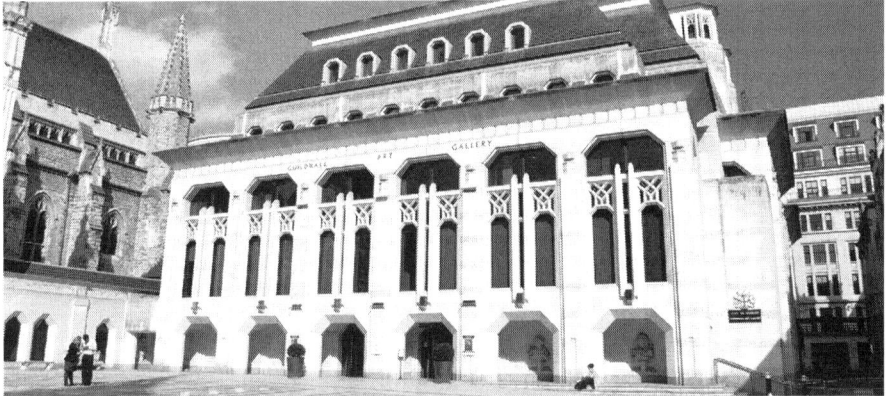

Nearest Station: St. Paul's
Address: Guildhall Yard, London, EC2V 5AE
Entry price: Free
Typical opening hours: Monday to Saturday from 10:00 to 17:00, and Sunday from 12:00 to 16:00
Phone: 0207 332 3700
Website: www.cityoflondon.gov.uk/things-to-do/visit-the-city/attractions/guildhall-galleries/Pages/guildhall-art-gallery.aspx

Established in 1886, the Guildhall Art Gallery today contains a range of paintings showing London's historical past. The paintings date as far back as the 1670s. Linked to the art gallery is London's Roman Amphitheatre which dates back almost 2000 years – the remains can be seen here today.

The permanent art collection is free admission, as is entry to the Roman Amphitheatres. Fees may apply for temporary exhibitions.

The Monument to the Great Fire of London

Nearest Stations: Monument, Bank and Cannon Street
Address: Fish St Hill, London, EC3R 8AH
Entry price: Adults – £4, Concessions – £2.70, Children (under 16) – £2
Typical opening hours: From 9:30 to 17:30 daily from October to March. There is a late closing at 18:00 from April to September. Last admission is 30 minutes before closing.
Phone: 0207 626 2717
Website: www.themonument.info

The Monument is a Doric column, measuring an astonishing 202 ft (62m) tall, making it the tallest freestanding stone column in the world. It was created to commemorate the Great Fire of London and it is located at the northern end of London Bridge.

The Monument contains a narrow staircase in the middle with 311 steps, which you can climb for an interesting view of the city. You do have to be in decent physical shape to make it up to the top – and it is not suitable for those who suffer from claustrophobia, despite the small windows on the way up. A mesh cage does restrict the view slightly at the top – this was added for safety reasons.

On the way out of The Monument you will be handed a certificate with a nice picture and some detail about the Fire.

Be sure to read the inscriptions at the base of the column which describe events around the fire: the south side describes King Charles II's actions following the fire, the east side describes how the fire started, and the north side contains a description of the damages caused by the fire.

Top Tip: You can get a combined ticket with the Tower Bridge Exhibition included for a discounted price.

Sky Garden

Nearest Station: Monument
Address: 20 Fenchurch St, London, EC3M 8AF
Entry price: Free
Typical opening hours: Monday to Friday from 10:00 to 18:00, and weekends from 11:00 to 21:00. Last entry is one hour before closing. Restaurants and bars are open until 1:00 on select nights.
Phone: 0207 337 2344
Website: www.skygarden.london

The Sky Garden at 20 Fenchurch Street, also known as the walkie-talkie due to its peculiar shape, has to be one of the most impressive free things to do in London. It is one of our favourite places to visit whatever time of the year.

The Sky Garden is a viewing gallery 35 floors above central London, with a huge inside area filled with plants. It is much more spacious than The Shard across the road, and also includes a small outside area. There's also the added advantage that you can get photos of The Shard itself, and you are closer to the city including the Tower of London and St. Paul's. The overall view, however, is not quite as impressive – whereas at The Shard you get the feeling of being on top of the world, it is more a sense of being just 'high up' here.

The Sky Garden is not just a viewing gallery, however, with three food and drink venues – Sky Pod Bar, Darwin Brasserie and Fenchurch Restaurant. Here you can dine, or enjoy a drink, and watch the world go by.

Tickets are limited to the gallery and are available to be booked three weeks in advance on the website. During peak periods, these dates sell out very quickly. 'Walk up' tickets are also available at no charge between 10:00 and 11:30, 14:00 and 16:30 on weekdays. You must bring a valid form of ID to enter Sky Garden.

Dining
Angler
Nearest Station: Moorgate
Address: 3 South Place, South Place Hotel, London, EC2M 2AF
Opening Hours: Lunch – Monday to Friday from 12:00 to 14:30. No lunch service on Saturday. Dinner – Monday to Saturday from 18:00 to 22:00. Closed on Sunday.
Phone: 0203 215 1260
Website: www.anglerrestaurant.com

Voted on Tripadvisor as one of the top 75 restaurants in London, Angler is a Michelin-starred fish-lover's fantasy. The food is exceptionally presented and deliciously seasoned, making this one of the best meals we have ever had in the city. The winter terrace allows you get to get beautiful views of the city year-round

Angler is on the pricier end of the scale with a la Carte dishes ranging for £19.50 to £38.50. A three-course lunch menu is available for £35. A 10-course tasting menu is available for £85. Reservations are accepted and highly recommended.

HKK
Nearest Stations: Liverpool Street and Moorgate
Address: 88 Worship Street, Broadgate Quarter, London, EC2A 2BE
Opening Hours: Monday to Saturday from 12:00 to 14:30, and 18:00 to 21:45. Closed on Sunday.
Phone: 0203 535 1888
Website: www.hkklondon.com

With an amazing ambiance, delicious food and impeccable service, HKK may just be the best high-end Chinese food in the city.

A la Carte dishes are priced between £12 and £38, with a tasting menu available for £88 with eight courses. Reservations are accepted.

Polo Bar
Nearest Station: Liverpool Street
Address: 176 Bishopsgate, Liverpool Street, London, C2M 4NQ
Opening Hours: Open 24/7
Phone: 0207 283 4889
Website: www.polo24hourbar.co.uk

Whatever time of day you visit The City, Polo Bar is happy to greet and feed you with its 24 hour opening times – something very unusual for London.

Polo Bar is a café and bar style environment, meaning it is much more laid back than other more formal options in The City, and serves comfort food. It serves generous portions and its industrial – yet spotless – interiors show how the area has become gentrified since this place first opened in 1959.

Breakfast is served all day and is priced between £7 and £10, with sandwiches and pancakes priced at £4 to £8. Lunch and dinner classics are £8.50 to £12, and there is even a budget afternoon tea here for under £10.

The Kitchen at Tower
Nearest Station: Tower Hill
Address: Byward Street, All Hallows by the Tower, London, EC3R 5BJ
Opening Hours: Monday to Friday from 8:00 to 17:30, Saturday from 9:00 to 17:30, Sundays and bank holidays from 10:00 to 17:30.
Phone: 0207 481 3533
Website: www.thekitchenattower.com

The Kitchen is one of our favourite hidden gems in central London for affordable eats. Located on the grounds of All Hallows by the Tower Church (parts of which date back to 700AD), The Kitchen serves British fare in leafy surroundings, and with friendly service that makes you feel like a local.

The early bird full English breakfast is just £6.50 before 11:00, whereas all-day meals are priced at under £11. The tea here is delicious and with the cakes on offer, you can even build your own mini afternoon tea here.

Accommodation

DoubleTree by Hilton – Tower of London
Nearest Station: Tower Hill
Address: 7 Pepys Street, London, EC3N 4AF
Telephone: 0207 709 1000
Website: http://doubletree3.hilton.com/en/hotels/united-kingdom/LONTLDI/

This modern 4-star hotel is well-located near the Tower of London, but is set far back enough from the busy road to effectively reduce any noise. Considering its location in the heart of The City, it provides great value for money for a mid-range hotel.

With a 24-hour fitness centre (but no pool), a stunning rooftop restaurant bar, and spacious rooms, we are big fans of this location. The hotel even has Europe's tallest green wall in the lobby. Rooms start at £138 per night.

Threadneedles, Autograph Collection by Marriott
Nearest Station: Bank
Address: 5 Threadneedle Street, London, EC2R 8AY
Telephone: 0207 657 8080
Website: www.hotelthreadneedles.co.uk

Located in a former bank building from the 1850s, this 5-star boutique hotel is an absolutely beautiful gem of a building with modern interiors and guest rooms, with classical touches. Service is excellent throughout the hotel and personable; it is quite a small location with only 66 rooms and 8 suites.

The hotel does not have a gym, but provides complimentary passes to one nearby (closed on Sundays). Wheeler's – an Oyster Bar and Grill – is a delightful restaurant to relax in. Rooms start at £212 per night.

Boundary Rooms & Suites
Nearest Station: Shoreditch High Street (Overground)
Address: 2-4 Boundary Street, London, E2 7DD
Telephone: 0207 729 1051
Website: www.theboundary.co.uk

This ex-Victorian warehouse has been converted into a French restaurant, rooftop bar and grill, and designer guest rooms. There are only 12 guest rooms, plus five suites, and each is unique; the smallest room measures a sizable 31 square metres (330 square feet). Rooms start at £276 per night.

London Bridge

The London Bridge area is located around the famous bridge and the extremely busy train station on the south side of the river. Here there are many different things to see including the tallest building in the European union – The Shard; Shakespeare's Globe Theatre; and the Tate Modern.

The current London Bridge is also available for your viewing pleasure, and Borough Market has delicacies to savour year-round.

Attractions
The View from The Shard

Nearest Station: London Bridge
Address: Railway Approach, London, SE1 9SG
Entry price: Adult – £30.95, Concessions – £25.95 to £26.95, Child (4 to 15) – £24.95.
Typical opening hours: From 25th October to 31st March – Sunday to Wednesday from 10:00 to 19:00, and Thursday to Saturday from 10:00 to 22:00. From 1st April to 24th October – Open daily from 10:00 to 22:00.
Phone: 0344 499 7222
Website: www.theviewfromtheshard.com

The Shard is an impressive structure. Standing at 1016-feet (310m) tall, it dominates London's skyline, and is the tallest building in the European Union. Towards the top of The Shard (at 244m high) is a viewing gallery. From here you can to see London's skyline up to 40 miles away (64km).

The experience starts as soon as you step foot in the building with the "kaleidoscopic" lifts transporting you to Level 69 in mere seconds. At the top you can explore the city from the indoor levels, or carry on up to the outdoor viewing platforms at Level 72 to get a true sense of how high up you are.
A complimentary multimedia guide and high-tech telescopes tell you about the history of the area, as well as details about key buildings and structures you can see today.

We have to admit, the views from the top are simply stunning and really give you a scale of London. It is a very impressive experience and feels very premium – the sense of being so high up is unlike anything else in the city.

Uniquely, they even offer a "Good Visibility Guarantee" which allows you to return within 3 months if you can't see select monuments during your visit due to bad weather.

As well as the standard single entry ticket, The View from The Shard also offers a "Day & Night" ticket which allows you to visit once during daytime, and again once the sun has set. This ticket is an upcharge of £10 per person.

Tickets for The View from The Shard are based on a 30-minute entry time slot. Once at the top, you can spend all long as you want admiring the view. Allow 45 minutes to an hour for the full experience.

Tate Modern

Nearest Stations: London Bridge and Southwark
Address: Bankside, London, SE1 9TG
Entry price: Free
Typical opening hours: Daily from 10:00 to 18:00, with a late closing at 22:00 on Friday and Saturday. Closed 24th to 26th December.
Phone: 0207 887 8888

Website: www.tate.org.uk/visit/tate-modern

Located in an old power station, the Tate Modern features a variety of permanent and temporary modern art exhibitions from around the world. This is an interesting museum that deserves a few hours of your time, and where there is always something new and thought provoking to see.

The museum's displays are free, but temporary exhibitions are paid admission.

The New Tate Modern opens on 17th June, 2016 and adds 60% more exhibition space.

Top Tip: Make your way to the café and restaurant at the top. Although it can be busy, the views towards St. Paul's and The City are stunning.

London Bridge
Nearest Stations: London Bridge and Monument
Address: London Bridge, London, EC4R 9EL
Entry price: Free
Typical opening hours: 24/7 – Public area

Up until the opening of Westminster Bridge in the 1860s, this was the only bridge to cross the river in central London. As such, it has gained somewhat of a mythical status, with several variations of the bridge having existed since the romans settled 2000 years ago. From timber bridges, to stone and now a steel and concrete structure, this bridge has always been a vital crossing for the city. The current bridge dates from 1974.

At the northern end of the bridge is The Monument to the Great Fire of London, with The Shard positioned on the other end.

The bridge has even inspired a nursery rhyme – "London Bridge is Falling Down". It is thought the song comes from the Viking attack in the early 11th century when the bridge was destroyed.

Today, London Bridge is a fantastic place to get perfectly framed photos looking down the river towards HMS Belfast and Tower Bridge.

HMS Belfast

Nearest Station: London Bridge
Address: The Queen's Walk, London, SE1 2JH
Entry price: Adults – £14.50, Children (5 to 15) – £7.25, Family – £25.45 to £38.15, Concessions – £11.60. All prices exclude a voluntary donation.
Typical opening hours: Daily from 10:00 to 17:00
Phone: 0207 940 6300
Website: www.iwm.org.uk/visits/hms-belfast

Learn all about WWII by stepping aboard a real ship used in battle. You can explore the nine decks of the ship, including the operations room, the living areas, engine rooms, missile rooms and much more.

The ship dates from 1938 and is a big hit, particularly with children. Allow at least two hours to see everything and to engage in the interactive exhibitions, as well as the live demonstrations and talks.

The London Bridge Experience & The London Tombs
Nearest Station: London Bridge
Address: 2 Tooley Street, London Bridge, London, SE1 2SY
Entry price: Adults – £24, Children (5 to 15) – £18
Typical opening hours: Daily from 10:00 to 17:00, with a late closing on weekends at 18:00. Summer season results in later closings, which vary day by day. Closed 25th and 26th December.
Phone: 0207 403 6333
Website: www.thelondonbridgeexperience.com

These two attractions take you back through London's horrible histories. The "London Bridge Experience" section of the tour is the more educational section, with live guides covering the history of London Bridge itself, ghosts, prisons, war, the Great Fire of London, and Jack the Ripper.

Then, through a vortex, you are transported to the "London Tombs" section, which is an altogether different experience. This is more like a horror maze type experience where the learning stops and the fear seems to never end as live actors make your experience one to remember.

Compared to the London Dungeon, which we covered earlier in this guide, this is a much less family-friendly experience once you enter the Tombs section. It is much more like a traditional haunted house style attraction in the second part. The first Experience section is educational, however. We do not recommend this attraction for young children.

Occasionally after hours' events are also offered. These are designed to be even more terrifying than the daytime shows.

Audio guides are available for international visitors to aid them with understanding the historical part of the attraction.

The Millennium Bridge

Nearest Stations: Southwark and St. Paul's
Address: Thames Embankment, London
Entry price: Free
Typical opening hours: 24/7 – Public area

The Millennium Bridge is one of the newest crossings of the River Thames and links The City of London (and St. Paul's Cathedral) with the Tate Modern and Shakespeare's Globe Theatre.

The bridge has been nicknamed the "Wobbly Bridge" due to an engineering disaster when it was first unveiled. As people crossed the bridge, their walking patterns created a force causing the bridge to sway. It had to be closed only a few days after opening in order to fix this issue, and re-opened two years later. Nowadays, it is a permanent non-moving structure, which is perfectly safe to cross.

The bridge allows you to get beautiful photos looking down the river towards Tower Bridge, and is also well-known for having been destroyed by Death Eaters in the sixth Harry Potter films.

Shakespeare's Globe Theatre Exhibition and Tours

Nearest Station: Southwark
Address: 21 New Globe Walk, Bankside, London, SE1 9DT
Entry price: Adults – £15, Concessions – £12.50 to £13.50, Children (5 to 15) – £9. Tickets include entry to both the exhibition and tour.
Typical opening hours: Exhibition – Daily from 9:00 to 17:30. Tours – Daily from 9:00 to 17:00. Closed 25th and 26th December.
Phone: 0207 902 1400
Website: www.shakespearesglobe.com

Explore this faithful reconstruction of Shakespeare's Globe Theater, opened in 1997, and designed to look as close to the original 1599 Globe as possible. Inside you can enjoy live Shakespearean shows, explore the exhibition, and tour the building itself.

The exhibition allows you to learn more about the Bard himself, including where he lived and who he wrote for initially. You also get an insight into the original Globe's construction and use. An audio guide is available for the exhibitions in several different languages, and is included in the entry cost.

The tours of the building tell you about the original Globe, the reconstruction process, and how it used to be a busy, real working theatre. Tours leave every 30 minutes.

Shows are also available to see at the Globe. These are covered later in this guide in our theatre section.

Dining
Vapiano
Nearest Stations: Southwark and London Bridge
Address: 90b Southwark Street, London, SE1 0FD
Opening Hours: Monday to Saturday from 11:00 to 23:00, Sunday from 11:00 to 22:00.
Phone: 0207 593 2010
Website: http://uk.vapiano.com

Vapiano is probably our favourite 'budget eat' in central London.

On the way in you will be given an RFID card, you then choose your seat wherever you want (this is quite a large location) and go to one of the stations to order your food. You can choose from pizza, pasta or salads – your food will be prepared fresh in front of you, to your specification in minutes, and you will take it away there and then. For pizzas you will be given a pager which will beep when your food is ready. You scan your card when you order your food, and pay on the way out.

This place is part fast food, part canteen, but with a restaurant-like quality and atmosphere. It might not be for everyone, but we love it. Portions are large, the meals are tasty, and prices are fair – the perfect combination. Pastas, risotto and pizzas run at £7 to £10.50 for a meal. Salads are priced between £5 and £10.

Our only qualm is that the waits for food can be long, due to the fact that everything is cooked to specification from scratch. Vapiano seems to be busy all day, every day, at all its locations. Vapiano has two more restaurants in London: on Wardour Street in Soho, and Great Portland Street by Oxford Circus station. Reservations are not accepted.

Aqua Shard
Nearest Station: London Bridge
Address: Level 31 – The Shard, 31 St. Thomas Street, London, SE1 9RY
Opening Hours: Restaurant: Breakfast – Weekdays from 7:00 to 10:30, weekends and bank holidays from 9:00 to 10:00. Brunch – Weekends and bank holidays from 10:30 to 15:30. Lunch – Weekdays (except bank holidays) from 12:00 to 14:45. Afternoon Tea – Weekdays (except bank holidays) from 15:00 to 17:00. Not available in December. Dinner – Daily from 18:00 to 23:00. The Bar: Daily from 12:00 to 01:00.
Phone: 0203 011 1256
Website: www.aquashard.co.uk

You have read about the viewing gallery at The View from The Shard a few pages back. Now, have lunch or dinner with with a view at Aqua Shard. Food is pricey, but the view, service and the delicious meal make it all worth it.

The breakfast set menu is priced at £29 per person. Lunch is £31 for two courses, or £34 for three. Afternoon tea is £42, and with champagne varies from £55 to £67. Dinner is served a la Carte with mains from £29 to £47, with some cheaper vegetarian options.

The views, as you can imagine, cannot be beaten. Reservations are accepted and highly recommended.

José Pizzaro Tapas
Nearest Stations: London Bridge and Borough
Address: 104 Bermondsey Street, London, SE1 3UB
Opening Hours: Monday to Saturday from 12:00 to 22:15, and Sunday from 12:00 to 17:15. Times listed are first and last orders.
Phone: 0207 403 4902
Website: www.josepizarro.com/jose-tapas-bar

This pricey Spanish location features mouth-watering dishes, and food is freshly sourced from the market, meaning that the menu really does change daily.

Seating is very limited, so be sure to turn up early for a spot. Reservations are not accepted for this restaurant.

Accommodation
Shangri La Hotel at The Shard
Nearest Station: London Bridge
Address: 31 St. Thomas Street, London, SE1 9QU
Telephone: 0207 234 8000
Website: www.shangri-la.com/london/shangrila

For a room with a view, look no further than the 5-star Shangri La Hotel inside The Shard. Spanning 19 floors, the 202 guest rooms each provide a unique view of London's skyline and access to the hotel's amenities.

An infinity pool, a fitness suite and valet parking are some of the services on offer. There are three excellent restaurants and bars within the hotel – LANG, TING, and GONG – the highest bar in London on the 52nd floor. Rooms start at £351 per night.

London Bridge Hotel
Nearest Station: London Bridge
Address: 8-18 London Bridge St, London, SE1 9SG
Telephone: 020 7855 2200
Website: www.londonbridgehotel.com

This 4-star hotel is located just moments from The Shard and Borough Market. The interiors are contemporary, and this is one of the few hotels not owned by a major chain. Amenities include an on-site gym with a sauna, the Londinium restaurant, and air conditioning in every room. As well as rooms and suites, serviced two-bedroom apartments are available for rental. Rooms start at £144 per night.

citizenM London Bankside
Nearest Station: Southwark and London Bridge
Address: 20 Lavington Street, London, SE1 0NZ
Telephone: 020 3519 1680
Website: www.citizenm.com

citizenM has been designed to offer luxurious rooms at the lowest prices possible, with ultra-modern interiors and an "XL King-size bed" in each room.

The hotel is perfect for those seeking quality without pretention; the lobby is set as a communal living room with a cafe and canteen open 24/7 for light meals. Rooms are for a maximum of two adults, and start at £109 per night.

Hyde Park, Notting Hill & Bayswater

Hyde Park adjoins with Kensington Gardens in central-west London and together make up over 600 acres of land. You could spend an entire afternoon, or longer, in the parks just seeing everything they have to offer. Surrounding the parks are the affluent areas of Notting Hill to the north, and Kensington to the south, Marble Arch and Park Lane are to the east with Mayfair there too. All the areas around the parks are also worth exploring for their unique characteristics.

The areas around Bayswater and Paddington are particularly popular with travelers on a budget due to the amount of "motel" style accommodation in this central area.

Attractions
Hyde Park and Kensington Gardens

Nearest Stations: Marble Arch, Hyde Park Corner, Knightsbridge, Lancaster Gate, Paddington and Queensway
Entry price: Free
Typical opening hours: 05:00 to 0:00 year-round for Hyde Park. 06:00 to dusk (between 16:15 to 21:45) for Kensington Gardens.
Website: www.royalparks.org.uk/parks/

Once Henry VIII's hunting grounds, today these two green areas combine to make the largest royal park in central London, spanning some 625 acres. Today, the two parks blend almost seamlessly and offer many sights.

The Serpentine is the largest manmade lake in London – here you can hire out a pedalo or a rowing boat and glide across the area. It is truly relaxing.

Boat hire is available from April to the end of October from 10:00 to sunset. The hourly rate is £12 per adult and £5 per child. Those fancying a dip may also want to swim at the park's lido.

For the truly warm days, you can sprawl on the grass or hire out one of the deck chairs to sunbathe. For the colder months of the year, why not pop into the park's several cafés? Numerous playgrounds and restaurants are dotted about the parks too.

The Serpentine Gallery and The Serpentine Sackler Gallery are both free admission and include art, architecture and temporary exhibitions. They are open from 10:00 to 18:00 Tuesday to Sunday.

Other highlights of the parks include The Princess Diana Memorial Fountain, the Diana Memorial Playground, and the Italian Gardens and Fountains in Kensington Gardens, which are worth a visit for their beautiful design. Many statues, fountains and memorials are also dotted around both parks. On the western end of the Park you will also find the Royal Albert Hall, as well as Kensington Palace.

Speakers' Corner on the north-east corner of Hyde Park, close to Marble Arch, is also another notable attraction. Here, on Sundays, people will gather to hear others exercise their right of free speech. You will find people stood on soapboxes talking about daily life, politics, the media and all manner of other subjects – and you can come and listen, for free of course. There are just three rules for the speakers: one cannot insult the monarch, incite a riot or beg for money. Anyone can participate by speaking, or simply watching.

Notting Hill
Nearest Station: Notting Hill
Typical opening hours: 24/7 – Public areas

Well-known for the 1999 film starring Hugh Grant and Julia Roberts, Notting Hill is every bit as charming in person as it is on the big screen. Every corner of this area holds a surprise, and the houses in this expensive area are to die for.

Each year in August, Notting Hill is home to the world's second-biggest carnival – Notting Hill Carnival – where London's West Indian communities gather to put on a street festival that is a joy to experience and filled with fantastic photo opportunities.

Notting Hill is also very well-known for its shopping. More information is available on this aspect later in the shopping section of this guide.

Portobello Road

Nearest Stations: Ladbroke Grove, Westbourne Park and Notting Hill Gate
Address: Portobello Road, London, W10 5TA
Typical opening hours: 24/7 – Public areas

This road, located in the heart of Notting Hill, is the world's largest antique market with over 1,000 dealers. However, you can come and visit this location any day of the week for a look at the bright, multi-coloured buildings and shops that are open year round.

More information is available on this area in our shopping section later in this guide.

Dining
Locanda Locatelli
Nearest Station: Marble Arch and Bond Street
Address: 8 Seymour Street, London, W1H 7JZ
Opening Hours: Lunch – Monday to Sunday from 12:00 to 15:00. Dinner – Monday to Thursday from 18:00 to 23:00, Friday and Saturday from 18:00 to 23:30, and Sunday from 18:00 to 22:15.
Phone: 0207 935 9088
Website: www.locandalocatelli.com

Amazing tasting Italian food is the name of the game here. The ambience is great, the food is delicious and the service is very attentive. Our only qualm is the pricing, which we feel is rather high. Pasta mains run from £18.50 to £22.50, whereas fish or meat dishes are £25 to £33.

With a dessert, a drink and tip added in (not to mention a starter), you can easily be looking at £50 per person here. Reservations are accepted.

Roti Chai
Nearest Station: Marble Arch
Address: 3 Portman Mews South, London, W1H 6HS
Opening Hours: Street Kitchen – Monday to Saturday from 12:00 to 22:30. Sunday from 12:30 to 21:00. Dining Room – Monday to Saturday from 17:00 to 22:30. Closed from 18:00 on 24th December and all day 25th December.
Phone: 0207 408 0101
Website: www.rotichai.com

Roti Chai, serving Indian fare, operates a dual food concept with a Street Kitchen café menu, as well as a more formal Dining Room. Both are equally delicious and cater to different types of dining experience.

Small dishes at the Street Kitchen are all under £5, buns are £6 to £7.50, and curry is affordable at £7.50 to £8.50. The Dining Room main courses are priced between £12.50 and £16. Reservations are accepted for the Dining Room area tables.

Lowry & Baker
Nearest Stations: Westbourne Park and Ladbroke Grove
Address: 339 Portobello Road, London, W10 5SA
Opening Hours: Monday to Saturday from 8:00 to 16:00, Sunday from 10:00 to 16:00
Phone: 0208 960 8534
Website: www.lowryandbaker.com

Lowry & Baker is hugely popular with both locals and visitors alike, meaning that you will need to get there early if you want to have lunch.

This is a café, which serves traditional sandwiches and cakes, but also offers more upscale choices such as "Flageolet beans on toast with spinach and homemade pesto".

The menu changes relatively frequently meaning that there is always something new and unique to try. This location is cash only.

Hereford Road
Nearest Stations: Bayswater and Notting Hill Gate
Address: 3 Hereford Road, Westbourne Grove, London, W2 4AB
Opening Hours: Monday to Saturday from 12:00 to 15:00, and 18:00 to 22:30. Sunday from 12:00 to 16:00, and 18:00 and 22:00.
Phone: 0207 727 1144
Website: www.herefordroad.org

Hereford Road is one of our favourite locations in all of London, and provides genuinely delicious food at ridiculously low prices. The kitchen is placed front and centre as you walk in, so you can see your food being freshly prepared.

The set lunch menu, available Monday to Friday, is amazing value at £13.50 for two courses, or £15.50 for three whilst including food such as fennel and onglet.

The A la Carte menu is also very reasonably priced with mains from £12 to £15.50 all day. Reservations are available.

Accommodation
Four Seasons Hotel Park Lane
Nearest Station: Hyde Park Corner and Green Park
Address: Hamilton Place, London, W1J 7DR
Telephone: 0207 499 0888
Website: www.fourseasons.com/london

This 5-star upscale hotel is located on the edge of Mayfair, just minutes from Hyde Park, Green Park, Buckingham Palace and the West End.

Amenities include a full-service spa, 24-hour fitness centre, and a multilingual concierge. A lounge/bar and exquisite restaurant complete the offerings, with the afternoon tea being a staple option. Service is exceptional and amongst the best we have received anywhere.

One of the unique features of the hotel is the first-come, first-served Rolls Royce chauffeur service within a 2-mile range of the hotel. Rooms start at £450 per night.

Park Grand London Paddington

Nearest Station: Paddington, Lancaster Gate and Bayswater
Address: 1-2 Queen's Gardens, London, W2 3BA
Telephone: 0207 298 9800
Website: www.parkgrandlondon.co.uk

This 4-star hotel boasts surprisingly modern interiors and, in our opinion, is one of the best values in London in terms of providing a good location, modern interiors and an attractive price. The hotel boasts an on-site restaurant and bar location, which is very affordable priced. Most rates include complimentary breakfast and Wi-Fi.

All the nearby tube stations are an 8-minute walk away. Rooms start at £88 per night.

Stylotel

Nearest Station: Paddington
Address: 160-162 Sussex Gardens, London, W2 1UD
Telephone: 0207 723 1026
Website: www.stylotel.com

Located just a few minutes from Paddington station, Stylotel is a 3-star ultra-modern budget hotel. The hotel is relatively small, with only 40 rooms, and 8 apartment suites with kitchenettes. The cheapest rooms are reasonably compact, but the value for money you get here is excellent in terms of how modern the hotel is and the location (a 15 minute walk will take you to Oxford Street for shopping and dining, for example).

Breakfast and Wi-Fi are included in most rates, and check-in is at a very early 1:00pm, which is handy for those arriving early into London. Rooms start at £72 per night.

Marylebone, Bloomsbury and Camden

Moving north of Oxford Street, you start to enter the areas of Marylebone, Bloomsbury and Camden. There are quite a few mainline railway stations in this area, including Marylebone, Euston, Kings Cross and St. Pancras.

Bloomsbury is an extremely nice area with many publishing houses located here, as well as the British Museum. Marylebone is in prime central London with Madame Tussauds and the Sherlock Holmes museum being the most well-known attractions here. Camden is a more alternative area known for its punk scene and food market, as well as the Zoo. The punk scene is less obvious here than ever before, however, as the area has gone a lot of gentrification in recent years.

Attractions
The British Museum

Nearest Stations: Holborn, Tottenham Court Road, Goodge Street and Russell Square
Address: Great Russell Street, London WC1B 3DG
Entry price: Free
Typical opening hours: 10:00 to 17:30 (daily) and 10:00 to 20:30 (Fridays)
Phone: 0207 323 8299
Website: www.britishmuseum.org

The British Museum is one the largest museums in the world, and houses over seven million artifacts relating to human history and culture. One of the most fascinating items on display is the Rosetta Stone, which was the key to us understanding Egyptian hieroglyphics. The cat mummies are also a must-see, as are the Egyptian sarcophagi, which are also on display.

At this museum you can travel across time from the age of Enlightenment back to the middle-eastern land of Mesopotamia in 6000 BC, and across the world from Italy to Japan.

There are also regular rotating free and paid exhibitions, which means that each visit to this magnificent place is different and equally fascinating.

Regent's Park

Nearest Stations: Baker Street, Regent's Park and Great Portland Street
Address: Chester Road, London, NW1 4NR
Entry price: Free
Typical opening hours: 05:00 to 17:00
Phone: 0300 061 2300
Website: www.royalparks.org.uk/parks/the-regents-park

Another of London's large parks, here you will find the Queen Mary's Rose Garden which every spring blooms with 12,000 roses. In the summer you will find the Open Air Theatre that performs all manner of productions, usually with at least one or two Shakespeare plays a year. The theatre performs from May to September with tickets usually costing £25 to £60. To the north of the park, you will find London Zoo – another notable attraction.

Behind Regent's Park, you will find Primrose Hill, which provides one of the most spectacular views of London's skyline from the top.

ZSL London Zoo

Nearest Station: Camden Town (15-minute walk)
Address: Regent's Park, London, NW1 4RY
Entry price: Adults – £25.50, Children (3 to 15) – £18.50, Concessions – £22.95
Typical opening hours: Open daily from 10:00 to 16:00 during winter, with closures as late as 18:00 in summer. Closed on Christmas Day.
Phone: 0207 449 6200
Website: www.zsl.org/zsl-london-zoo

London Zoo is regarded as the world's oldest zoo, having opened in 1828. Housing over 19,000 animals of 800 different species, this is the largest collection of animals in London. Whether you want to see seahorses in the aquarium, the lions on their African plains or the reptile enclosure where they filmed the first Harry Potter film, there is something here for everyone. Plus, there are a large variety of shows and talks throughout the day, as well as several dining locations to enjoy.

Brand new for 2016, is the Gir Lion Lodge, an opportunity to stay the night inside the zoo in the new Land of the Lions area. Your stay includes breakfast and dinner, as well as zoo entry for two days and special guided events. Adults-only and family-friendly nights are offered. Rooms can accommodate a maximum of two adults, plus children. The opportunity will be available from May to December 2016, with prices ranging from £378 to £558.

Madame Tussauds

Nearest Station: Baker Street
Address: Marylebone Road, London, NW1 5LR
Entry price: Adults – £34, Children – £29.50
Typical opening hours: Monday to Friday from 9:30 to 17:30 and weekends from 9:00 to 18:00. During peak periods opening hours extend from 8:30 to 18:00 daily.
Phone: 0871 894 3000
Website: www.madametussauds.com/London/

This famous waxwork museum was the first "Madame Tussauds" location in the world. Marie Tussaud, born in 1761, made wax masks before public executions in France. Just after the French Revolution she brought her collection of masks to England in an exhibition. The attraction moved to its current home in 1884.

Today, Madame Tussauds is where you can find true-to-life wax representations of famous figures throughout history – real and imaginary. Inside, there is everyone from David Beckham to Lady Gaga, and The Queen to Albert Einstein.

Recent additions include a Bollywood section and even another with YouTube stars. A Marvel area and Star Wars locations are also available as of early 2016 – these areas are changed up every few years to keep the attraction's offerings fresh.

The attraction also includes a scare zone called the Chamber of Horrors, which can be skipped if you wish. A classic slow-moving ride through the sights of London is a fun end to your journey.

The Sherlock Holmes Museum

Nearest Station: Baker Street
Address: 221b Baker Street, London, NW1 6XE
Entry price: Adults – £15, Children – £10
Typical opening hours: Daily from 9:30 to 18:00. Closed on Christmas Day.
Phone: 0207 224 3688
Website: www.sherlock-holmes.co.uk

221b Baker Street is undoubtedly one of the most famous addresses in the world. Home of the fictional character Sherlock Holmes, you can now visit the address, which has been converted into a museum. Explore this Victorian house and move from Sherlock's room to Dr. Watson's and keep an eye out for all the items dotted around, which reference parts of the books.

As the location is a regular-sized house, and was not built to be a visitor attraction, you will often see a queue line outside the building to get in. The inside will usually take you less than half an hour to see and given the entry price, this may be best suited for only the most devoted Sherlock fans.

Harry Potter's Platform 9 ¾ & Shop

Nearest Station: King's Cross St. Pancras
Address: Kings Cross Station, Euston Road, London, N1 9AL
Entry price: Free
Typical opening hours: Daily from 05:00 to 01:00 for the station and photo opportunity. The shop is open from 8:00 to 22:00 Monday to Saturday, and 9:00 to 21:00 on Sunday.
Website: www.harrypotterplatform934.com

The station itself is beautiful from the outside, particularly after its multi-million re-development which concluded in 2013.

However, it's what is inside the station that counts – for Harry Potter fans at least. Fans of the Wizarding boy will remember that King's Cross Station (and more specifically Platform 9 ¾) is where the Hogwarts Express departs from.

Due to the success of the films and books, a photo opportunity with a luggage trolley was put in place between platforms 9 and 10. As this was causing congestion on the platforms, the photo op has now been relocated to the left of the large departure boards in the waiting hall. This is a very popular spot year-round, so there is a queuing system for the photo opportunity. You can take your own photos or get a professional paid one done here.

To the left of this is a shop that sells all manner of Harry Potter merchandise – from Hogwarts scarves to wands, and key-rings to copies of the books.

British Library

Nearest Station: King's Cross St. Pancras
Address: 96 Euston Road, London, NW1 2DB
Entry price: Free
Typical opening hours: Monday to Thursday from 09:30 to 20:00, Friday from 09:30 to 18:00, Saturday from 9:30 to 17:00, and Sunday from 11:00 to 17:00. The Treasures Gallery exhibition closes at 18:00 on Mondays, and with the building on all other days.
Phone: 0330 333 1144
Website: www.bl.uk

The British Library is the official national library of the United Kingdom. According to its number of catalogued items, it is regarded as the largest library in the world. It contains a collection of over 170 million items in many languages from different sources.

The British Library is not just books – it is stocked with documents in digital and print form. They include music recordings, databases, stamps, maps, patents, drawings, magazines and more.

This library even contains historical items and manuscripts dating back to 2000 BC, and the Treasures Gallery exhibition contains gems such as the 800-year-old Magna Carta, and important document that states that everyone should be subject to the law (including royals) and have the right to a fair trial.

The Wallace Collection

Nearest Station: Bond Street
Address: Hertford House, Manchester Square, London, W1U 3BN
Entry price: Free
Typical opening hours: Daily from 10:00 to 17:00. Closed 24th to 26th December.

Phone: 0207 563 9500
Website: www.wallacecollection.org

The Wallace Collection contains some of the most fascinating pieces of art in all of London. The Great Gallery inside has been described as "the greatest picture gallery in Europe." Highlights of the collection include Frans Hals' "The Laughing Cavalier" dating from 1624, Parisian royal furniture dating from the 1700s, and Ruben's stunning "The Rainbow Landscape" from 1636. Admission is free to all exhibitions, including temporary ones.

Abbey Road Studios

Nearest Station: St. John's Wood
Address: 3 Abbey Road, London, NW8 9AY
Typical opening hours: 24/7 – Public area
Phone: 0207 266 7000
Website: www.abbeyroad.com

Visit the famous zebra crossing where The Beatles were photographed for their Abbey Road album cover. Now you too can recreate the scene. You are also free to take photos of the outside of the historic Abbey Road Studios, but the inside is a real working studio for professionals only. Be sure to visit the shop if you would like some Beatles memorabilia.

There's a live web cam pointed towards the crossing so you watch others cross when your back home.

Surprisingly, for the most part, drivers are rather accommodating of visitors taking the extra few seconds to get a picture whilst crossing – but, be careful!

London Canal Museum

Nearest Station: King's Cross St. Pancras
Address: 12 New Wharf Road, London, N1 9RT
Entry price: Adults – £4, Children – £2, Concessions – £3, Family – £10
Typical opening hours: Open Tuesday to Sunday from 10:00 to 16:30. Late closing on the first Thursday of each month at 19:30. Closed on Mondays, except bank holiday Mondays. Last admission is 30 minutes before closing.
Phone: 0207 713 0836
Website: www.canalmuseum.org.uk

Fans of waterways and canals will enjoy this place. The London Canal Museum tells the story of the creation of London's canals in the late 18th century. See what the living conditions were like on board the canal boats, then how their use declined, and how subsequently they became seen as a form of leisure.

Learn how locks work and more with the interactive exhibitions. The museum's second theme is ice – you can learn how resourceful the Victorians were with it.

Finally, the museum runs canal boat trips with commentary through the Islington Tunnel on Regent's Canal. These are an extra £4 or so per person on top of museum admission, and run on select dates – check the website for details. Pre-booking is highly recommended; this can be done online.

Dining
Bento Café
Nearest Station: Camden Town
Address: 9 Parkway, London, NW1 7PG
Opening Hours: Sunday to Thursday from 12:00 to 22:30, and Friday & Saturday from 12:00 to 23:00
Phone Number: 020 7482 3990
Website: www.bentocafe.co.uk

For some of the best Japanese food in London, Bento Café in Camden Town is a fantastic option. Mains such as the Salmon Teriyaki and the Ebi Mentaiko run between £7.50 and £19. Side dishes are £3 to £7 each on average. The sushi and sashimi platters are fresh and are a good option to share, whereas the 'all day bento boxes' are fantastic value meals for one priced at £10.50 to £14.

A few doors down is sister restaurant Bento Ramen, which specialises in ramen noodles and dim sum.

Dishoom
Nearest Station: King's Cross St. Pancras
Address: 5 Stable Street, Kings Cross, London, N1C 4AB
Opening Hours: Weekdays from 8:00 to 23:00, with a late closing at 0:00 on Thursday and Friday. On Saturdays the location is open from 9:00 to 0:00, and on Sundays from 9:00 to 23:00.
Phone: 0207 420 9321
Website: www.dishoom.com

For authentic, delicious Indian fare, there is no better place than Dishoom. Unusually for London, this restaurant is actually open throughout the day, and even serves breakfast! Cooked breakfasts and naan rolls are priced between £5 and £8.50. For lunch, small plates run at £2.50 to £5, grilled dishes are £6.50 to £12, curries are £8 to £9, salads and vegetarian dishes are all under £10. Select dishes are also available to takeaway from breakfast to 17:00.

As well as this King's Cross location, Dishoom's other restaurants are just off Carnaby Street, in Covent Garden, and in The City. Reservations are accepted.

Chiltern Firehouse
Nearest Station: Baker Street
Address: 1 Chiltern St, Marylebone, London, W1U 7PA
Opening Hours: Breakfast – Monday to Friday from 7:00 to 10:30, weekends from 0:00 to 10:30. Brunch – Weekends only from 11:00 to 15:00. Lunch – Monday to Wednesday to 12:00 to 14:30, Thursday and Friday from 12:00 to 15:00. Dinner – Monday to Wednesday from 17:30 to 22:30, Thursday to Sunday from 18:00 to 22:30.
Phone: 0207 073 7676
Website: www.chilternfirehouse.com

This old firehouse has now been converted into a luxury hotel, complete with a fantastic restaurant to boot. Nuno Mendes, Michelin-starred chef, heads up the operation. With a focus on what is in season, the menu changes regularly, and has an American flair. This place is a favourite of London-based, and international, celebs.

The venue is beautiful, but beware that this premium experience does carry a cost. Portions are not the largest. Mains are £20 to £44 at both lunch and dinner. Reservations are accepted, and almost a necessity due to popularity.

Accommodation
St. Pancras Renaissance Hotel
Nearest Station: King's Cross St. Pancras
Address: Euston Road, London, NW1 2AR
Telephone: 0207 841 3540
Website: www.stpancraslondon.com

This stunning building has only recently come out of a lengthy refurbishment, now cementing it is a one of London's top 5-star luxury hotels. The hotel describes itself perfectly: combining "Victorian splendour with contemporary style and impeccable service". The building has so much history that tours by Blue Badge guides are available at an extra charge.

As far as dining, you are spoilt for choice: with a bar and restaurant, a lounge, a terrace overlooking the train station, and an upscale dining establishment. An in-house spa adds to the amenities on offer.

Rooms are relatively large, starting at 25 square metres (270 square feet) on the smallest end of the scale. Prices start at £189 per night.

Ibis London Euston St Pancras

Nearest Station: Euston and Euston Square
Address: 3 Cardington Street, Kings Cross, London, NW1 2LW
Telephone: 020 7388 7777
Website: www.accorhotels.com/gb/hotel-0921-ibis-london-euston-st-pancras/index.shtml

Ibis is a well-known brand that provides well-priced rooms. This particular location is next door to Euston station, and 15 to 20 minutes' walk from King's Cross and St. Pancras stations.

An in-hotel restaurant and bar provide somewhere to eat, and as you would expect from a budget brand there is no on-site fitness suite or pool. Rooms are basic and make good use of the space, though bathrooms are small. Rooms start at £79 per night.

YHA London St. Pancras

Nearest Station: King's Cross St. Pancras
Address: 79-81 Euston Road, London, NW1 2QE
Telephone: 0845 371 9344
Website: www.yha.org.uk/hostel/london-st-pancras

This is the only hostel we are listing in the guide, as we consider it to be the best in London. Just a short walk from the tube, YHA London St. Pancras provides basic, but comfortable, beds for a bargain price.

There is a café-bar area that serves light snacks, the staff are friendly and the British Library is just across the road.

Single beds start at £16, with private rooms from £59 per night. Family rooms are also available from £55 per night.

Further Afield

Sometimes it is worth going a bit further out of the centre of the city to experience some unique attractions that you just can't get in central London. Here, we have listed attractions that are worth making that journey. Some attractions are further out than others, but none will require more than a 45-minute train journey. Others are just 10 or 15 minutes from central London.

We do not list any restaurants or accommodation options in this section as we do not feel it is worth making a trip out of the centre specifically to dine. It is also much more practical to remain in central London in terms of accommodation, where you can find affordable places to stay in the heart of the action.

Attractions
Kew Gardens and Kew Palace

Nearest Station: Kew Gardens
Address: Royal Botanic Gardens, Kew, Richmond, TW9 3AB
Entry price: £15 per adult, £3.50 per child. Tickets include entry to the gardens and palace.
Typical opening hours: The Gardens are open year-round (except 24th and 25th December) from 10:00 to 16:15 in low season, and open up to 19:30 in the summer. Last entry is 30 minutes before closing. The Palace is open in the summer season – in 2016 this is from 2nd April to 27th September between 10:30 and 17:30.
Phone: Kew Gardens – 020 8332 5655, Kew Palace – 0203 166 6000
Website: www.hrp.org.uk/kew-palace and www.kew.org/visit-kew-gardens

Kew Gardens, opened in 1840, contains the largest collection of living plants in the world. With over 30,000 distinct types of plants and over seven million plant specimens, the scale of the Gardens cannot be understated.

This UNESCO World Heritage Site features several buildings to explore, plus it boasts a treetop walkway to give you a unique perspective on the woodland below. Tours are offered throughout the day.

Entry to Kew Gardens includes entry to the gardens themselves, plus Kew Palace (built in 1631 as Samuel Fortrey's country abode), the Royal Kitchens and Queen Charlotte's Cottage (a retreat from her 'mad' husband George III). The Cottage is only open to visitors at weekends and on Bank Holidays from April to September.

Richmond Park and Bushy Park

Nearest Station: Richmond
Address: Richmond, Greater London
Typical opening hours: 24/7 – Public area. Richmond Park has limited opening hours in November and February during the deer cull – at this time the park is open from 7:30 to 20:00. Bushy Park also has limited opening hours in September and November – they are 8:00 to 22:30, Monday to Friday.

Both of these rather large parks are free to enter, and they feel like you are a world away from a major capital city. Richmond Park spans 2360 acres, whereas Bushy Park measures some 1099 acres. They are the two largest royal parks in London and are a short walk from each other.

At Richmond Park, you can enjoy the Isabella Plantation which contains exotic plants; wildlife such as 650 wild deer, trees and birds; King Henry's Mound with views to St. Paul's Cathedral; as well sports and leisure activities. At Bushy Park, you can see the Diana Fountain; the tranquil Upper Water Lodge Gardens; the USAAF memorial; the wildlife, and more.

Greenwich

Nearest Station: Cutty Sark (DLR)
Address: Greenwich, London, SE10
Entry price: Free
Typical opening hours: 24/7 – Public area. Museum and attraction opening times vary.

Greenwich is one of the gems of London that we still think is underappreciated to this day. Despite being just minutes away from central London on the tube, it still has very much of a village feel to it, with plenty of green space and has fantastic sightlines of central London.

Although we have listed Greenwich here as one place, there are many things to do in the area. Highlights in this area include the National Maritime Museum, Cutty Sark, Queen's House and Old Royal Observatory.

The National Maritime Museum is the largest museum of its kind in the world with 10 free galleries to explore. Admission is free.

The Cutty Sark is the world's only surviving tea clipper and dates from the 19th century. You can step aboard the ship and learn all about its history, as well as the restoration work to make it viewable by the public today. Admission is £12.15 per adult, £6.30 per child and £10.35 for concessions.

The Queen's House is under refurbishment at the time of writing, and will reopen in summer 2016, with a major art exhibition to mark its 400th anniversary. It is today used as an art gallery, and dates from the 17th century.

The Meridian Line & Historical Royal Observatory at the top of the hill provide spectacular views of the city and Canary Wharf. Here you can take a photo with the prime meridian that divides the world's eastern and western hemisphere and is the basis of GMT (Greenwich Mean Time). Admission is £9.50 for adults, £5 for children, and £7.50 for concessions. The Astronomy Centre at the Royal Observatory nearby is free admission and contains interactive exhibitions related to the stars and planets.

Finally, the Old Royal Navy College contains beautiful grounds, as well as the Greenwich Visitor Centre, the stunning Painted Hall (which has been described as 'the Sistine Chapel of the UK') and the beautifully quaint Chapel of St Peter and St Paul.

All the museums listed here open from 10:00 to 17:00 daily, with last admission at 16:15 or 16:30; they are all closed 24th to 26th December.

Greenwich Royal Park surrounds many of the area's museums and is a great place to sunbathe, relax or have a picnic during the warmer months.

One of the more picturesque ways of getting to Greenwich is via a river cruise from central London to Greenwich – allow at least an hour for this journey. Another faster and more economical way of getting to Greenwich is via the Docklands Light Railway (DLR), which also provides interesting views along the way – you can get the DLR at Bank or Tower Gateway in central London. The journey time is about 25 minutes.

Queen Elizabeth Olympic Park

Nearest Stations: Stratford International and Stratford
Address: London, E20 2ST
Entry price: Free for the park. Venues may charge entry.
Typical opening hours: The park is open 24/7. It is a public area. Venues have their own operating times.
Phone: 0800 072 2110
Website: www.queenelizabetholympicpark.co.uk

The Queen Elizabeth Olympic Park is a public park and sports complex in East London. It was built for the Olympic and Paralympic Games held in summer 2012. Originally called the Olympic Park, it today offers cultural and sports amenities, as well as many outdoor areas

As well as enjoying the park's open public spaces, there are numerous playgrounds for children, a climbing wall, gardens and riverside walkways, public art displays, cafes, and more.

The Olympic Stadium is a wonder to behold and is right in the centre of the park. When its redevelopment is completed in 2016, it will be home to West Ham United Football Club, and British Athletics.

The Velopark, Hockey and Tennis Centre, and the Aquatics Centre allow you to cycle, bat and swim in the same place that Olympians have played at a world level. These are accessible to all members of the public for a charge. Check for times, session dates and pre-requirements online.

The Arcelormittal Orbit, the UK's tallest sculpture, also dominates the skyline in the park and provides an observation deck at 80 metres in height. On a clear day you can see for up to 20 miles. On the way up, you take a lift to reach the top, but from 24th June 2016 (for an additional charge) you will be able to make your descent on the world's tallest and longest tunnel slide, instead of a lift. Tickets for the viewing platform are £12 per adult and £7 per child. Concessions are £10.

Check for events taking place at the park online before visiting as these are plentiful throughout the year.

The park is just 15 minutes from central London, yet feels a world away. It is pure tranquility and you may just be able to spot some well-known monuments in the skyline, such as The Shard.

New: Stratford and The Queen Elizabeth Olympic Park were recently moved from Zone 3 on the London Undergound to the Zone 2/3 boundary meaning that if you have a Zone 1 and 2 Travelcard you can travel to Stratford at no extra cost. Oyster and Contactless fares are now cheaper too, and cost the same as any journey in Zone 1 and 2.

Warner Bros. Studio Tour London – The Making of Harry Potter

Nearest Station: Watford Junction
Address: Studio Tour Drive, Leavesden, WD25 7LR
Entry price: Adults – £35, Children – £27, Family – £107
Typical opening hours: Opening hours vary significantly, from 10:00 to 18:00 in low season, to 09:00 to 22:00 in high season. Last admission is usually three to four hours before closing time. All tours are pre-booked. Closed 14th to 18th November and 25th to 26th December 2016.

Phone: 0845 084 0900
Website: www.wbstudiotour.co.uk

Harry Potter fans should make The Warner Bros Studio Tour a must-see attraction during their visit. Inside you will step foot into the Great Hall, see Hagrid's Hut, see wizarding wands, see the real Hogwarts Express and a scale model of Hogwarts Castle, visit Diagon Alley and other film sets, see props and costumes, and much more.

There are both inside and outside sections on this tour, and you will need at least three hours to get a good overview of everything inside. You can either guide yourself or use one of the audio guides, which are available at an additional charge.

If you are using public transport to reach this attraction, you will need to get off at Watford Junction station on the Overground. From here, a regular shuttle bus service runs to the Studios at a cost of £2.50 return per person. Alternatively, there is also a shuttle bus service available directly from central London – more information can be found online. If you are arriving by car, parking is free.

Tickets for this attraction must be bought in advance and are not available for purchase on-site. You will select an entry time slot before arrival. We strongly recommend booking as far in advance as possible as tickets are limited and they do regularly sell out – even during the off-peak season.

Hampton Court Palace

Nearest Station: Hampton Court (National Rail). The Underground does not serve this area.
Address: East Molesey, Surrey, KT8 9AU

Entry price: Palace, Maze and Garden tickets are priced at £16.50 for adults, £8.25 for children, £14 for concessions and £42.50 for families. Individual maze and Garden tickets are also available.

Typical opening hours: From 25th October to 24th March 2016 (winter) – Open daily from 10:00 to 16:30. From 25th March to 29th October (summer) – Open daily from 10:00 to 18:00. Last entry is one hour before closing. Closed 24th to 26th December.

Phone: 0203 166 6000

Website: www.hrp.org.uk/hampton-court-palace/

Dating back over 500 years, Hampton Court Palace is a spectacle to behold. Although much of the original palace is now gone, the current building still dates back to the late 1600s.

Inside the palace you can see England's last medieval hall, the stunning Chapel Royal, the Cumberland Art Gallery, visit William III's State Apartments, and much more. Once you step outside, you can explore the stunning gardens and step foot inside the maze, where you can try to find your way out.

Wimbledon Lawn Tennis Museum and Tours

Nearest Stations: Southfields and Wimbledon Park
Address: Church Road, Wimbledon, London, SW19 5AE
Entry price: Museum only: Adults – £13, Children – £8, Concessions – £11; Museum and Tour: Adults – £24, Children – £15, Concessions – £21

Typical opening hours: Open daily from 10:00 to 17:00 or 17:30 (depending on season). Last admission is at 16:00 or 17:00. Tours do not run between 13th June and 15th July. Additionally, the museum is only open to Championship Ticket Holders between 27th June to 10th July. The museum is closed 1st January, 26th June, 11th & 12th July, and 24th to 26th December in 2016.
Phone: 0208 946 6131
Website: www.wimbledon.com/en_GB/museum_and_tours/index.html

Tennis fans are in luck with this whole museum dedicated to the great sport. Museum visits include access to the museum itself with an audio guide, as well as entry to the 3D cinema, and a 10-minute guided tour of Centre Court. Inside the museum, visitors can see the Championship Trophies up close, learn how the game has evolved since 1877, and see how the Victorians dressed when they played. The museum usually takes about an hour to see.

For those wanting a more in-depth experience, tours with a qualified Blue Badge Guide are available which last 90 minutes; these also include museum admission.

More information on the actual tennis games played here is available in the sports section.

Windsor Castle

Nearest Stations: Windsor & Eton Riverside (National Rail) and Windsor & Eton Central (National Rail). The Underground does not serve this area.
Address: Windsor, Windsor and Maidenhead, SL4 1NJ
Entry price: Adults – £20, Concessions – £18.20, Children (5 to 16) or Disabled visitors – £11.70, Family – £51.70

Typical opening hours: Open daily from 9:45 to 17:15 from March to October. From November to February, Windsor Castle closes one hour earlier. Last admission is 16:00 and 15:00 respectively.
Phone: 0207 766 7304
Website: www.royalcollection.org.uk/visit/windsorcastle

If you are going to make a trip to one castle outside of central London, make it Windsor Castle. This is the oldest and largest inhabited castle in the world and it is a magnificent sight to behold, dating back to the 19th century.

Windsor Castle is where The Queen spends a substantial amount of her time, including many weekends, and a month over the Easter period. To this date the castle has been home to 39 monarchs, spanning back over 900 years.

Your visit to Windsor Castle will include: The State Apartments where the Royal Family often host events for organisations they support; Queen Mary's Dolls' House, the largest doll's house in the world made on a scale of 1:12; The Semi-State Rooms (open from September to March only); and St. George's Chapel.

In the same vain as at Buckingham Palace, there is also a Changing the Guard ceremony at Windsor Castle. The ceremony takes place at 11:00 within the Castle grounds Mondays to Saturdays from April until the end of July, and on alternate days for the rest of the year. There is no Changing the Guard on Sundays. A provisional schedule is available online.
Be sure to take in one of the Precinct Tours, led by the Wardens, which last 30 minutes and give you an overview of the castle's history. A multimedia tour handset can be picked up near the entrance to guide you through the castle – this is available in nine different languages, including English. A special child-friendly multimedia tour option is also available in English only.

Legoland Windsor

Nearest Stations: Windsor & Eton Riverside (National Rail) and Windsor & Eton Central (National Rail). The Underground does not serve this area. You will need to then catch a bus to the theme park.
Address: Winkfield Road, Windsor, SL4 4AY
Entry price: Adults – £50.40, Children – £46.20. Parking is £5.
Typical opening hours: Open on select days in March, April, May, September and October. Open daily from June to August. Also open on 5th November. Park opening times vary from 10:00 to 17:00 off=peak days, and 10:00 to 19:00 during the summer peak.
Phone: 0871 222 2001
Website: www.legoland.co.uk

Operated by Merlin Entertainments, Legoland Windsor is a theme park dedicated to kids aged 2 to 12, though anyone can go along and enjoy it of course. There are over 55 attractions on the 150-acre site.

Explore areas such as Miniland where you can see models of famous UK landmarks; jump on a train or rollercoaster; hop onto a water ride; or battle mummies on an interactive laser shooting ride – all while surrounded by millions of LEGO bricks!

Legoland is not open year-round and closes over winter. See their website for more details.

Shopping

London is a shopping capital, and British brands sell well on all four corners of the globe. As you can imagine, no matter where you turn in London, you will find somewhere to spend your money.

Whether you are looking for luxury items in Knightsbridge or Mayfair, or high street shopping on Oxford Street, you are sure to find something that will suit your taste.

Camden Market

Opening Hours: Daily from 10:00 to 18:00.
Nearest Station: Camden Town

Camden Market is one experience that visitors to London cannot miss. From small market stalls to bigger permanent stores, those looking to grab something unique to taste or to take home must make a stop in Camden. If you are a fan of vintage, however, you will get even more joy from your visit!

There are, in fact, six different areas to the market, each with its own character. Explore Inverness Street Market, Stables Market, Camden Lock Market, Buck Street Market, Camden Lock Village and the Electric Ballroom. There are a mix of both indoor and outdoor areas.

The market is most active on Sundays, although trading is also done on Saturdays. A more limited amount of trading takes place on weekdays. Weekends are definitely the time to visit, however, and the market attracts around 100,000 visitors each and every weekend. If you are coming for food, you can get this year-round with stalls representing almost every corner of the world.

Borough Market

Opening Hours: Lunch market only – Monday and Tuesday from 10:00 to 17:00. Full market – Wednesday and Thursday from 10:00 to 17:00. Friday from 10:00 to 18:00. Saturday from 8:00 to 17:00. Closed on Sunday.
Nearest Stations: London Bridge and Southwark

Nestled just a minute's walk from London Bridge station, Borough Market is definitely worth a visit for foodies.

The Central London food market is known as one of the oldest and largest markets in London. It is stocked with food sourced from all the continents of the world.

Borough is steeped in history. It has been the site of food markets for over 1000 years, but the market on the current site has been present since the 18th century.

Oxford Street

Opening Hours: Monday to Saturday 9:00 to 20:00, Sunday 12:00 to 18:00. Some shops open later.
Nearest Stations: Marble Arch, Bond Street, Oxford Circus and Tottenham Court Road.

Oxford Street is Europe's busiest shopping street (with over half a million visitors daily), and is home to over 300 different stores. Oxford Street contains all sizes of shop, including many large flagship department stores such as John Lewis, House of Fraser, and Marks and Spencer.

Oxford Street is perhaps most notable for Selfridge's, located to the Western end of the road. Selfridge's, founded in 1909, is the second largest department store in London, second to Harrods. It was founded by Harry Gordon Selfridge, an American who coined the phrase 'the customer is always right'.

Also on Oxford Street, you will find brands ranging from United Colors of Benetton to Nike Town and Primark. Unique to Oxford Street, is the fact that most of the shops are affordable, big high-street names. New Bond Street and Old Bond Street run perpendicular to Oxford Street; these are the main luxury shopping roads in London, with big international brands, as well as London corporations.

Measuring 1.2 miles (just under 2km) in length, you can easily spend an entire day on this one road alone, visiting each and every shop.

Hours listed in this section are general shopping hours, with many large shops staying open later until 21:00 or 22:00 from Monday to Saturday. Due to Sunday trading laws, large shops can only open for six hours on Sundays. Smaller shops on Oxford Street may still be open later than 18:00 on this day.

Regent Street

Opening Hours: Monday to Saturday 9:00 to 20:00, Sunday 12:00 to 18:00. Some shops open later daily.
Nearest Stations: Oxford Circus and Piccadilly Circus.

Regent Street is yet another popular shopping road in central London. It links to Oxford Street at Oxford Circus. Generally speaking, this location features more of a mix of pricing styles than Oxford Street – here there are more affordable stores stood next to the likes of Burberry and Swarovski. It is by no means, a luxury shopping destination in the same way that New and Old Bond Street are.

Regent Street was the world's first shopping street, having been built in the 1820s and rebuilt 100 years later. The facades of all the buildings are lined in Portland Stone, with few exceptions. Today, the street is managed by The Crown Estate, and it was originally designed for the Prince Regent (who later became George IV).

Notable locations on the street include:
* The Apple Store, located near Oxford Circus, was the largest of the brand's shops in the world up until 2010;
* Hamley's, a toy store established in 1760 in High Holborn as "Noah's Ark" and moved to its current location in the 1880s. Hamley's is seven floors selling all manner of toys. It is the world's oldest and largest toy shop.
* Liberty, just off Regent Street on Marlborough Street, is a luxury department store. The building's façade is in a beautiful mock Tudor style.
* BBC Broadcasting House is the headquarters of the British Broadcasting Corporation.

Running parallel to the west of Regent Street is Saville Row, the best place to buy tailor-made suits in London.

Carnaby Street runs parallel to the east of Regent Street. Once the heart of fashionable shopping in the Swinging Sixties, the street is still a well-known name. Today, this street is pedestrianised and is home to 150 retailers, and 50 dining locations and bars.

Westfield – London (White City) & Stratford City

Opening Hours: London White City location – Monday to Saturday from 10:00 to 22:00. Sunday from 12:00 to 18:00. Stratford City location – Monday to Friday from 10:00 to 21:00. Saturday from 9:00 to 21:00. Sunday from 12:00 to 18:00.
Nearest Stations: Shepherd's Bush, Wood Lane and Stratford.

Looking at the previous listings in this shopping section, you would be forgiven for thinking that Londoners are bigger fans of shopping streets than shopping centres. However, the prospect of air-conditioned, indoor shopping where everything is in one place has become more and more appealing.

Today, Westfield owns two large shopping centres, on the eastern and western ends of central London. Both are excellent choices for shopping and feature national and international brands. The differentiation between the two shopping centres is minimal.

The London (White City) location features 372 stores over five levels, whereas the Stratford City location features 350 stores over three levels. The Stratford City location is the largest urban shopping centre in Europe. Both locations feature a multi-screen cinema, and the Stratford City location also has a casino and a bowling alley. In addition, the Stratford City Westfield is directly connected to the Olympic Park.

Although shops close at a set time at both Westfield shopping centres, the restaurants and other entertainment options are open later.

Knightsbridge and Harrods

Opening Hours: Monday to Saturday from 10:00 to 21:00. Sunday from 11:30 to 18:00. Hours are for Harrods. Individual shops' hours vary.
Nearest Stations: Hyde Park Corner and Knightsbridge.

Knightsbridge is known as a luxury shopping and residential district. It is mostly located in the Royal Borough of Kensington and Chelsea. With Hyde Park on one side, and Belgravia to the other, Knightsbridge is perfectly placed in the lap of luxury.

Notable brands found in the area include Ferrari, Harvey Nichols, Rolex, Aquascutum and Porsche Design.

The best known store in the area, however, is Harrods. Founded in 1834, this luxury department store is the *de facto* destination for the rich. It is the biggest department store in Europe, with 330 departments and retail space of one million square feet (90,000 m^2). It is worth exploring to see the incredible variety of things on offer, and the beautiful food court has to be seen to be believed.

Covent Garden

Opening Hours: Monday to Friday from 10:00 to 20:00, Saturday from 9:00 to 20:00, Sunday from 12:00 to 18:00.
Nearest Station: Covent Garden

Covent Garden is a popular visitor destination, with shopping in almost every direction you look and many pedestrianised areas. The area is in the heart of Theatreland, and therefore is perfect for some post- or pre-theatre shopping and dinner.

Covent Garden started life in 1654, where an open vegetable and fruit market was developed in the southern part of the square. The square is still the heart of the area but shops are now on all the surrounding streets too. Under the square's central roof, you will find a split-level set of shops with many small, independent boutiques present.

Big international brands are also on the square, such as the likes of Apple, Barbour, Chanel, Disney, Ladurée, GNC, and Pandora.

We love the ambiance of Covent Garden and because it is a whole area, instead of just one street, the crowds are more spread out making it feel more relaxing in our opinion.

The times listed are general opening times and individual shop hours vary.

Piccadilly

Opening Hours: Monday to Friday from 10:00 to 20:00, Saturday from 9:00 to 20:00, Sunday from 12:00 to 18:00.
Closest Station: Green Park and Piccadilly Circus

Piccadilly gets its name from the white frilly collars that were once sold in the area – the Piccadills. Today, Piccadilly is still a commerce street with many small, unique shops in the heart of the West End, and links to Regent Street via Piccadilly Circus, as well as Bond Street. Many of the shops in the area hold Royal Warrants; these are seals of approval from senior members of the Royal Family who shop there.

Notable shops along the road include:
* Fortnum and Mason, established in 1707, with very lavish classic British interiors it sells luxury goods and has its own tea room.
* Burlington Arcade with its small boutique shops is beautiful. The Piccadilly Arcade across the road is similar, yet more simple, in style.
* Hatchards, a bookshop that has been present on the road since 1797, is a treasure trove inside and regularly holds high-profile signings.
* Waterstones is a modern book shop spanning six floors, with over 200,000 unique titles. This is the largest bookshop in Europe and is open to 22:00 every day, except Sunday. It even has its own restaurant and bar on the top floor, called 5th view. There is also a café in the store.

The Ritz Hotel and the Hard Rock Café are also located on Piccadilly.

The times listed are general opening times and individual shop hours may vary.

Notting Hill and Portobello Road

Opening hours: Daily from 9:00 to 17:00. The main market is on Saturdays.
Nearest Stations: Ladbroke Grove, Westbourne Park and Notting Hill Gate

Situated in the Royal Borough of Kensington and Chelsea, Notting Hill is a district in London. It is well known for hosting the annual Notting Hill Carnival, and the weekly Portobello Road Market. It is one of London's most affluent areas.

Notting Hill is now globally known as an attractive area with restaurants, large Victorian townhouses and high-end shopping. This was not the case before the early 1980s, when rents in the area were relatively cheap.

Notting Hill is home to Portobello Market (on Portobello Road), a street market which is divided up into sections. You will find antiques, fruit and veg, new goods, clothes and fashion, and second hand items sold at the market. The antiques are undoubtedly what the market is most famous for. The market takes place on Saturdays and starts to get busy from 9:00 onwards, and starts winding down between 17:00 and 19:00. Some trading does take place on other days of the week, mostly from the permanent shop fronts, but Saturday is the day to come.

Brick Lane

Opening Hours: Shops open daily from 9:00 to 19:00. The main market takes place on Sundays from 10:00 to 17:00.
Nearest Station: Shoreditch High Street (Overground) and Aldgate East (Underground)

Brick Lane is a fashionable, up-and-coming destination in Central-East London, and the heart of the British Bangladeshi community. Many people call it Banglatown, and it is widely known for its curry houses.

The street was formerly known as Whitechapel Lane, however it got its new name from the manufacturing of brick and tile during the 15th century.

Brick Lane is filled with fashionable shops which are open daily, as well as an incredible amount of street art including works from Banksy and D*Face.

Brick Lane Market is a popular destination on Sundays and specialises in second-hand goods, including clothes, furniture, books, and much more. Trading here takes place on Sundays from 10:00 to 17:00.

Bicester Village Shopping Outlet

Opening Hours: Monday to Friday from 9:00 to 19:00. Saturday from 9:00 to 20:00. Sunday from 10:00 to 19:00, with select shops open from 12:00 to 18:00 only due to Sunday Trading Laws.
Nearest Station: Bicester Village (National Rail)

This shopping outlet is actually located in Oxfordshire, outside of London. Access can be obtained by taking a train from London Marylebone station to Bicester Village station. The journey takes 46 minutes on the train, with return train tickets priced at £25.

Bicester Village (pronounced "bister") houses 131 stores including several of the world's leading fashion brands like Bally, DKNY, Diane Von Furstenberg, Salvatore Ferragamo, Mathew Williamson, Smythson, Anya Hindmarch, Hugo Boss, Church's and many other brands. There are also dining establishments to take a break between all the shopping.

This is a popular destination and hosts over 6 million shoppers every year. The outlets are open year-round, and are particularly popular on bank holidays.

Music, Arts and Nightlife

As well as shopping and museums, culture buffs have no shortage of live performances in London either. The West End is the heart of the theatre district with musicals, comedies and dramas galore. If live music is more your scene, that is catered for too. Those wanting to party away into the night will also find solace in London's nighttime scene.

Musicals

Musicals have been a staple in London for hundreds of years and there is a wide array to choose from.

Matilda: The Musical
Playing at: Cambridge Theatre, Earlham Street, London, WC2 9HU
Run time: 2 hours and 45 minutes with one intermission
Website: www.matildathemusical.com

Matilda: The Musical is based on Roald Dahl's novel of the same name. Matilda has already been turned into a famous film, and now it is a wildly successful musical too. Matilda on Broadway won seven Olivier awards in 2012; in London this popularity continues. It is easy to see why: with catchy songs, great decors and a story we can all relate to in some way or another, Matilda captures the hearts of theatregoers each and every night.

The Phantom of the Opera
Playing at: Her Majesty's Theatre, 57 Haymarket, London, SW1Y 4QL
Run time: 2 hours 30 minutes with a 15-minute intermission
Website: www.thephantomoftheopera.com/london

An Andrew Lloyd Webber production that tells the tale of a fascinating love story, unlike anything you have ever seen before. With incredible scriptwriting, memorable songs and incredible set changes, it is no wonder that this show has now been performing for 30 years at Her Majesty's Theatre.

Book of Mormon
Playing at: Prince of Wales Theatre, Coventry Street, London, W1D 6AS
Run time: 2 hours 30 minutes with a 15-minute intermission
Website: www.bookofmormonlondon.com

The Book of Mormon is a satirical musical based on The Church of Jesus Christ of Latter-day Saints. The story follows two Mormon missionaries to Uganda and the struggles they face as AIDS, poverty, war and famine impede their activities. The musical is hilarious, with clever lyrics, and won four Olivier awards in 2014.

We Will Rock You
Playing at: Dominion Theatre, 268-269 Tottenham Court Road, London, W1T 7AQ
Run time: 2 hours and 40 minutes with a 15-minute intermission
Website: www.wewillrockyou.co.uk

We Will Rock You is based on a book written by Ben Elton, and the songs of Queen. The musical follows the story of Bohemians who strive to bring back freedom. Despite encountering huge criticism during its introduction, the musical has become a sensation and is popular with audiences from around the world. It is a fun night out that is sure to get everyone involved.

Jersey Boys
Playing at: Piccadilly Theatre, 16 Denman Street, London, W1D 7DY
Run time: 2 hours and 40 minutes with one intermission
Website: www.jerseyboyslondon.com

Jersey Boys is told as if it were a documentary, describing the life and times of The Four Seasons – a rock n' roll group during the 1960s. The show is divided into "four seasons". Each season contains a vivid explanation of events by one of the band's members.

Billy Elliot
Playing at: Victoria Palace Theatre, 126 Victoria Street, London, SW1E 5EA
Run time: 2 hours and 40 minutes with a 15-minute intermission
Website: www.billyelliotthemusical.com

Billy Elliot: The Musical is based on the movie of the same name, which in turn is inspired by a 1935 novel by A. J. Cronin about the miner's strike. The story follows Billy, motherless, and who sells gloves and shoes. Having been in London since 2005, the musical has won many awards including a coveted Olivier for Best New Musical.

Les Miserables
Playing at: Queens Theatre, 51 Shaftesbury Avenue, London, W1D 6BA
Run time: 2 hours and 50 minutes with a 20-minute intermission
Website: www.lesmis.com

Les Miserables, also widely known as Les Mis, is based on the novel of the same name by Victor Hugo. The musical is set in France during the 19th century and recounts the tale of a French peasant named Jean Valiean who seeks salvation after spending nineteen years behind bars. The musical was originally unveiled in French, with its English lyrics later being composed by Herbert Kretzner.

Stomp
Playing at: Ambassadors Theatre, West Street, London, WC2H 9ND
Run time: 1 hour and 40 minutes
Website: www.stomplondon.com

Stomp is a percussion group with roots in Brighton. The group use everyday objects and their bodies to make music. The original Stomp has been performing since the summer of 1991, and you too can go along and join in the fun.

Thriller Live!
Playing at: Lyric Theatre, 29 Shaftesbury Avenue, London, W1D 7ES
Run time: 2 hours and 10 minutes with a 20-minute intermission
Website: www.thrillerlive.com

Thriller Live! is a concert-style experience that celebrates Michael Jackson, and the music of The Jackson 5. In 1988, the show started as a fan club based in Britain. The huge following of the show led to an annual tribute concert for Michael Jackson. Now, this is the closest thing to the real deal. There is no acting, it is just song after song. Though the idea of being seated may seem odd for a concert, by the end of the show you *will* be up and dancing.

Charlie and the Chocolate Factory
Playing at: Theatre Royal Drury Lane, Catherine Street, London, WC2B 5JF
Run time: 2 hours and 30 minutes with one intermission
Website: www.charlieandthechocolatefactory.com

Charlie and the Chocolate Factory is based on Roald Dahl's novel from 1964, as well as taking inspiration from the films that have since been produced. With catchy songs, fantastic sets, and beautiful décor inside the world's oldest working theatre, this is sure to be a night out to enjoy.

Mamma Mia!
Playing at: Novello Theatre, Aldwych, London, WC2B 4LD
Run time: 2 hours and 35 minutes with a 15-minute intermission
Website: www.mamma-mia.com

Mamma Mia is another West End favourite, and retells the story of a bride-to-be who tries to find which of three men is her real father. Of course, all this is just an excuse to get as many ABBA songs into one musical as possible. Those tracks include: Dancing Queen, Super Trouper, Take a Chance on Me, The Winner Takes It All, SOS, and a host of others.

The Lion King
Playing at: Lyceum Theatre, 21 Wellington Street, London, WC2E 7DA
Run time: 2 hours and 40 minutes with a 15-minute intermission
Website: www.thelionking.co.uk

The Lion King is one of the most popular animated movies of all time, and Disney has taken the opportunity to turn it into a musical. First premiered in 1997 on Broadway, the musical made its way to the West End in 1997. Instead of having people dress up as the film's characters, intricate marionettes and puppets are used to retell the story in a way never seen before.

Wicked
Playing at: Apollo Victoria Theatre, 17 Wilton Road, London, SW1V 1LG
Run time: 2 hours and 45 minutes with a 15-minute intermission
Website: www.wickedthemusical.co.uk

Wicked is the untold story of the Wicked Witch of the West from the popular tale "Wizard of Oz". Here you discover why the Witch is so mean, and what an interesting story it is. With incredibly funny songs, a fantastic script and sets to astound, this is one of the best shows we have ever seen.

Sunny Afternoon
Playing at: Harold Pinter Theatre, 6 Panton Street, London, SW1Y 4DN
Run time: 2 hours and 45 minutes with one intermission
Website: www.sunnyafternoonthemusical.com

Sunny Afternoon retells the story of Ray Davis's life and the creation of band The Kinks, who enjoyed a string of chart-topping successes. Going where other musicals don't dare, Sunny Afternoon exposes the loves and losses that the band encountered on their road to fame, and delivers an emotional punch that will warm your heart and leave you buzzing. Sunny Afternoon was the winner of the coveted 2015 Olivier Award for Best New Musical.

Plays

London's theatre scene isn't all singing and dancing…

The Woman in Black
Playing at: Fortune Theatre, Russell Street, London, WC2B 5HH
Run time: 2 hours with one intermission
Website: www.thewomaninblack.com

The Woman in Black is a horror stage play performed by only two actors. The play follows the story of a lawyer obsessed with a curse that he believes has been cast over him and his family by the spectre of a Woman in Black. He engages a young actor to help him tell his terrifying story and exorcise his fear. As they reach further into his darkest memories, they find themselves caught up in a world of eerie marshes and moaning winds.

Get ready to be creeped out, as the small theatre adds to tense atmosphere. Having been in London for over 25 years, this is one show that is here to stick around, terrifying audiences for years to come.

The Mousetrap
Playing at: St. Martin's Theatre, West Street, London, WC2H 9NZ
Run time: 2 hours and 15 minutes with a 15-minute intermission
Website: www.the-mousetrap.co.uk

The Mousetrap, written by Agatha Christie, first opened in 1952 and has been consistently running since then. With over 25,000 performances, and a run time of 64 years, it is the longest running modern play anywhere in the world. In typical Agatha Christie style, this is a case of trying to guess "whodunit".

Theatre-goers are asked not to reveal the ending before leaving the theatre in order to keep the enjoyment for future audiences.

The Play that Goes Wrong
Playing at: Duchess Theatre, Catherine Street, London, WC2B 5LA
Run time: 2 hours and 5 minutes, with a 20-minute intermission
Website: www.theplaythatgoeswrong.com

The Play That Goes Wrong is based on the antics of the Cornley Polytechnic Drama Society who is trying to stage a 1920s murder mystery, and everything that can go wrong, does. With many genuine laugh out loud moments, it is no wonder that the play won 'Best New Comedy' at the 2015 Olivier awards.

Dance, Opera and Other Performances

Whether you fancy a bit of ballet, contemporary dance or opera, London's performance scene is thriving.

Shakespeare Globe Theatre

Nearest Stations: London Bridge and Southwark
Address: 21 New Globe Walk, Bankside, London SE1 9DT
Phone: 0207 902 1400
Website: www.shakespearesglobe.com

Shakespeare's Globe Theatre is a reconstruction of the magnificent, original Globe Theatre. The current structure stands around 230 meters from the original structure. Ever since it was reopened in 1997, the Shakespeare Globe Theatre has staged plays every summer. Tours of the building are also available.

London Coliseum (English National Opera)

Nearest Station: Leicester Square
Address: St Martin's Lane, London, WC2N 4ES
Phone: 020 7836 0111
Website: www.eno.org

The London Coliseum is a theatre situated at St. Martin's Lane in Central London. It was constructed as one of the most luxurious and largest variety theatres in London, and opened in December 1904. Today it is primarily used for opera, as well as being the London home of the English National Opera.

Royal Opera House
Nearest Station: Covent Garden
Address: Bow Street, London, WC2E 9DD
Phone: 0207 240 1200
Website: www.roh.org.uk

Situated in Covent Garden, the Royal Opera House is a venue used for various types of performing arts. It houses several groups like The Royal Ballet, The Orchestra and The Royal Opera. It was originally called the Theatre Royal and served as a playhouse for the first century of its history. Tours are available at this location.

The Peacock Theatre
Nearest Stations: Holborn and Covent Garden
Address: Portugal Street, London, WC2A 2HT
Phone: 0207 863 8000
Website: www.sadlerswells.com

Situated in Westminster near Aldwych, the Peacock Theatre has a capacity of 999-seats. It is owned by the London School of Economics and Political Science, and forms an integral part of its campus.

The theatre is used for public talks, political speeches, conferences, open days and lectures. It is also often used to host ballet, dance performances, award ceremonies, pop concerts and conferences.

The Roundhouse
Nearest Station: Chalk Farm
Address: Chalk Farm Road, London, NW1 8EH
Phone: 0300 678 9222
Website: www.roundhouse.org.uk

The Roundhouse is an old railway engine shed located in Chalk Farm. Just before World War II, the building fell into a state of disuse. In 1964, it was reopened as a venue for performing arts. After being empty for years, performing arts returned to this building after it was purchased by a local businessman in 1996. It is now one of the most unique venues in London with a capacity of 1,700 people.

Music and Arts:
The O2 Arena
Nearest Station: North Greenwich
Address: Peninsula Square, London, SE10 0DX
Phone: 0208 463 2000
Website: www.theo2.co.uk

Initially called the Millennium Dome at opening – and home to a major exhibition – The O2 is now a dining venue with a cinema, and crucially an arena with a seating capacity of 20,000. It is one of the main music venues in London, and has the second highest capacity in the UK, after The Manchester Arena. It is the world's busiest arena by a large margin, with 1.8 million ticket sales in 2014.

The easiest way to reach the venue is by tube via North Greenwich station on the Jubilee Line, with a travel time of only 15 to 20 minutes from Central London. Another popular transportation option is the Thames Clippers River Express from major piers in Central London every 20 minutes.

Wembley Arena

Nearest Station: Wembley Park
Address: Arena Square, Engineers Way, London HA9 0AA
Phone: 0208 782 5566
Website: www.ssearena.co.uk

Once a swimming pool, Wembley Arena is now a premiere music venue located right next to the behemoth Wembley Stadium. It is the second largest indoor arena in London, after the O2, with 12,500 seats.

With good transport links, and being located only half an hour from central London, Wembley Arena is a solid choice for bands playing in the city.

Royal Albert Hall

Nearest Stations: South Kensington, Gloucester Road and High Street Kensington
Address: Kensington Gore, Kensington, London SW7 2AP
Phone: 0207 589 8212
Website: www.royalalberthall.com

The Royal Albert Hall is a multi-purpose concert hall in South Kensington. The Hall has a seating capacity of almost 5,300 for performances by rock bands or pop stars, ballets or operas. The building dates from 1871, when Queen Victoria and Prince Edward opened it.

It has been the residence concert venue for The BBC Proms every summer since 1941; these are daily classical music performances, usually at affordable prices.

Dubbed "The Nation's Village Hall", the Royal Albert Hall is one of UK's most important and most treasured buildings.

As well as the large, paid events in the main hall, there are also Free Music Fridays. These take place in Verdi, the Italian restaurant within the building – a different artist, or series of artists, plays every week. Tours of the building are also available; more information on this is available in the neighbourhood guide section of this book.

Barbican Centre

Nearest Stations: Barbican
Address: Silk Street, London, EC2Y 8DS
Phone: 0207 638 4141
Website: www.barbican.org.uk

The Barbican Centre is a performing arts centre in the City of London, and the largest of its kind in Europe. The Centre hosts classical and contemporary music concerts, theatre performances, film screenings and art exhibitions. The Barbican Hall is home to the London Symphony Orchestra and the BBC Symphony Orchestra.

Personally, we are not fans of the building's layout or architecture but it is a Grade II listed building meaning it may not be demolished, extended, or altered without special permission from the local planning authority. That ensures that the Barbican is set to stick around for quite a while.

The interiors are pleasant and there is always something different going on, but be sure to check what is showing in advance before visiting to avoid disappointment.

Southbank Centre

Nearest Stations: Waterloo
Address: Belvedere Road, London, SE1 8XX
Phone: 0207 960 4200
Website: www.southbankcentre.co.uk

The Southbank Centre is one of Britain's top arts institutions and a large arts complex. The 21-acre estate runs from County Hall to Waterloo Bridge, and is Europe's largest center for the arts, averaging 3 million visitors per year. Southbank Centre consists of three main buildings: the Queen Elizabeth Hall, Royal Festival Hall and the Purcell Room.

Also in the complex are the Hayward Gallery, Jubilee Gardens, the Saison Poetry Library and the Queen's Walk.

With a seating capacity of 2,500, the Royal Festival Hall was officially unveiled in 1951 as part of the Festival of Britain. Today it is a world-renowned concert hall for music, dance and literature.

The Hayward Gallery features visual arts across all periods and has a very diverse set of exhibitions. Past shows featured works of Leonardo da Vinci, Eduard Munch and French Impressionists.

The Southbank Centre welcomes a wide range of creativity and culture – music, arts, classical, rock, pop, jazz, dance, yoga, performances, spoken word, poetry, visual arts, painting, sculpture, architecture, and more. Not only a live music venue, it is also a solid teaching and training ground

The Southbank Centre has four resident orchestras: the London Philharmonic Orchestra, the Philharmonic Orchestra, the Orchestra of the Age of Enlightenment, and the London Sinfonietta.

The Queen Elizabeth Hall, Purcell Room and Hayward Gallery closed in September 2015 for two years of essential repair and maintenance.

The British Film Institute (BFI) Southbank

Nearest Stations: Waterloo
Address: South Block, Belvedere Rd, London, SE1 8XT
Phone: 0207 928 3232
Website: www.bfi.org.uk

A four-screen cinema venue showing over 2,000 classic and contemporary films each year, with film seasons, director and actor retrospectives, and extended runs of cinema classics. View over 1000 hours of free film and TV in the Mediatheque, visit the library and film shop, and enjoy two of the Southbank's best restaurant bars.

Founded in 1933, BFI cares for the BFI National Archive, the largest film archive in the world containing 50,000 fiction movies, over 100,000 non-fiction ones and around 625,000 television programs. This library of moving pictures is not exclusively British. The British Film Institute aims to celebrate British and international filmmaking success through exhibitions, publishing, DVD releases, festivals, and education.

Pricing is: Adults – £10.65, Concessions – £8.35, Children (Under 16) – £6. If you are 25 or under and register online, you can get tickets for any showing for just £3 with valid ID, subject to conditions.

Nightlife

Despite the fact the trains stop running early, and most shops are closed by 9:00pm, London does indeed have a nightlife scene – and a roaring one at that!

From relaxing bars, to pubs to while away a few hours, to the pounding music from the club nights, London's character changes after the sun sets, and the partying goes on well into the early hours of the morning in many locations.

Bars
Opium
Nearest Station: Leicester Square
Address: 16 Gerrard Street, London, W1D 6JE
Phone: 0207 734 7276
Website: www.opiumchinatown.com

Pop in for the best dim sum in town, and incredibly creative cocktails with unique Asian-inspired ingredients. Expect to pay £11 to £15 for a cocktail here, £5 to £6 for a beer, wine prices vary.

Vista at The Trafalgar
Nearest Station: Charing Cross
Address: 2 Spring Gardens, Trafalgar Square, London, SW1A 2TS
Phone: 0207 870 2900
Website: www.thetrafalgar.com/vista-homepage/

The name says it all here: Vista. It is indeed the view you come for when visiting this rooftop bar overlooking Trafalgar Square. This is a seasonal venue that operates during Spring and Summer only, and serves light food in the evenings.

It is also usually open on the 31st December to ring in the New Year and see the fireworks. There is a £5 cover charge for this venue, with a minimum spend also applicable.

Cahoots
Nearest Station: Piccadilly Circus and Oxford Circus
Address: 13 Kingly Street, London, W1B 5PG
Phone: 0207 352 6200
Website: www.cahoots-london.com

Cahoots is one of our favourite themed bar concepts with the interiors resembling an old Underground train – just with more space to maneuver, and even the staff are in character. There are a wide variety of cocktails on offer, which are all fantastic, and they also usually host live music acts. This is a popular location and table reservations (for a 2-hour slot) are a must – yes, for a bar.

Clubs
Koko
Nearest Station: Mornington Crescent
Address: 1a Camden High Street, London, NW1 7JE
Website: www.koko.uk.com

This Camden club is popular because of its affordable entry prices, large selection of acts, and interesting layout inside. It was once a theatre and you can tell as soon as you step in the venue. We are not huge fans of the prices charged for drinks, however!

The venue hosts regular events other than standard club nights, such as concerts throughout the week. There are very few places to rest, though, so be prepared to stand for a while. If you do need to sit down, look out for the leather sofas at the back of the main room.

The Electric Ballroom
Nearest Station: Camden Town
Address: 184 Camden High Street, London, NW1 8QP
Phone: 0207 485 9006
Website: www.electricballroom.co.uk

A well-known venue in London, The Electric Ballroom provides well priced drinks, a fantastic ambiance, and regular national and international acts. It comes highly recommended for a night out and has a good balance between a club and music venue. The top area has seats for those needing to chill out for a bit.

Fabric
Nearest Station: Farringdon and Barbican
Address: 77a Charterhouse Street, London, EC1M 6HJ
Phone: 0207 336 8898
Website: www.fabriclondon.com

Fabric is a well-known nightclub in London, and is extremely popular so get there early. This is a place for people who really like their music and will appreciate the fantastic sound system. Expect to pay at least £20 for entry – sometimes closer to £30, but they regularly get big name DJs. Book your tickets in advance, if you can, to reduce your wait getting in.

Pubs
The Lock Tavern
Nearest Station: Chalk Farm and Camden Town
Address: 35 Chalk Farm Road, Camden, London
Phone: 0207 482 7163
Website: www.lock-tavern.com

This pub is well-sized, with a large beer garden and roof terrace, which makes it perfect for a sunny day. Food is generally good, and drink prices are acceptable for the location. There are occasional live music acts too, which also add to the ambiance.

Ye Olde Cheshire Cheese
Nearest Station: Chancery Lane and St. Paul's
Address: 145 Fleet Street, London, EC4A 2BU
Phone: 0207 353 6170

If you want history, there is no better pub to pay a visit to in The City. This pub was rebuilt in 1667 and stepping foot inside is like going back 350 years. Go downstairs into the authentic drinking areas deep underground and be reminded how much shorter people were as you duck down the steps. We love the ambiance inside, and the food and drink are decent too! Even Samuel Johnson used to drink here!

The Cross Keys
Nearest Station: Covent Garden
Address: 31 Endell Street, London, WC2H 9BA
Phone: 0207 836 5185
Website: www.crosskeyscoventgarden.com

An absolutely tiny, intimate location that is very pretty inside (and outside). Beer and food are good, but get there early for a table or seat. It is also conveniently located in the West End if you would like to carry on your night in one of the many bars or clubs in the area.

Getting back after a night out
Do be aware that London's Underground system stops running from the city centre around midnight, with night buses and taxis being the main ways to get around after that. Alternatively, you could party away into the night until the first trains reach the center of London around 6:00.

If you are returning home on a night out in a taxi, either hail a black cab or book a mini-cab such as Uber (by calling or via an app) – hopping into a mini-cab in the spur of the moment is illegal and unsafe. Remember if your minicab is not pre-booked, there is no trace of your journey should anything go wrong.

Sport

What better way to round your trip off in London than with a bit of live sport? London has plenty of choice with sporting arenas dedicated to football, tennis, rugby and cricket, as well as multi-use venues.

The best place to get tickets for any sport is to check online at the official stadium websites, which will link to authorised sellers. Not using the official sales channels, and visiting ticket resellers, may either mean paying too much, getting fake tickets, or both. Many locations also sell tickets directly at the box office on-site.

For tours of the locations featured below you can either pre-purchase tickets online, or buy them on the day of your visit. Tickets will generally be cheaper in advance, and you can avoid the disappointment of turning up and finding that tours are all sold out. Stadium tours selling out is common, particularly during summer months and school holidays.

Wembley Stadium

Nearest Station: Wembley Park
Address: Wembley, London, HA9 0WS
Phone: 0844 980 8001
Website: www.wembleystadium.com

Wembley Stadium is a 90,000-seater football stadium in north-west London. It is the largest stadium in the UK, the second largest in Europe, and opened in 2007, replacing the old stadium. Wembley hosts the FA Cup Final, the England national football team, and other big football matches like the UEFA League.

Be sure to look out for the bronze statue of Bobby Moore at the stadium entrance, which commemorates England's 1966 World Cup win. The stadium is located about 30 minutes from central London by tube or car.

As well as sports events, the stadium has also staged music performances from renowned artists such as Oasis, U2 and Coldplay.

Aside from the matches played here, you can tour the inside of the stadium year-round, except on Wembley event days. Experience the awesome behind-the-scenes feel and action as your tour guide leads you to the changing rooms, the press conference room, the VIP club for a spectacular panorama of the stadium, the royal box, the exhibitions, and the stadium store.

Please note that from Monday 29 February 2016 to Sunday 31 July 2016, tours of Wembley Stadium will not include the Manager's Benches or the Royal Box. A VIP tour option is also available. Tours last 75 minutes and depart hourly from 10:00 to 15:00 and are priced at £19 per adult, £11 per child (under 16), with concessions paying £11. A family ticket is £45.

Lord's Cricket Ground

Nearest Station: St. John's Wood
Address: St John's Wood Road, London, NW8 8QN
Phone: 0207 616 8500
Website: www.lords.org

Lord's Cricket Ground is the definitive home of cricket in London, and is situated in St. John's Wood. Established in 1814, this 28,000-seater venue hosts international test matches and major local competitions. Lord's is also where the oldest sports museum is, the MCC Museum contains the precious Ashes urn from 1882. 2014 marked its 200-year anniversary. The present Lord's is the third incarnation.

If you are not visiting for a sporting event, you can still tour the cricket ground year-round. Tickets to the tour include entry to the MCC Museum. Tours last 100 minutes and run 7 days a week. You will see the Honours Board, sit in the dressing rooms, enter the Long Room, and of course see the Ashes Urn. The Lord's Tour is very popular, especially during the summer months, and tours are often fully booked in advance. Prices are £20 for adults, £15 for over 60s, £12 for children (5 to 15) and students, and £49 for a family. Tours do not run on major match days.

The MCC Museum is open on all match days for visitors with a ticket for that day's play.

Emirates Stadium – Arsenal F.C.

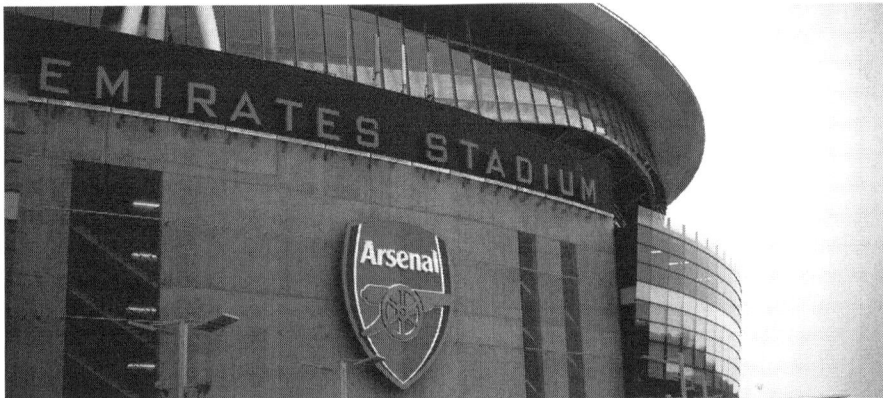

Nearest Station: Arsenal
Address: Hornsey Road, London, N7 7AJ
Phone: 0207 619 5003
Website: https://bookings.arsenal.com

The Emirates Stadium is the third biggest football stadium in England with a capacity of 60,272 seats, after Wembley and Old Trafford.

Like many other sports locations, the Emirates Stadium is open to visitors year-round through tours, and even has a museum.

At the museum you can immerse yourself in the history of Arsenal F.C. by following the story of the club's formation in 1886 right through to the present day. You can also see famous shirts and boots in the exhibition. Tickets are £8 for adults, and £5 for children (under 16) and concessions.

A self-guided audio tour is another option. Here you can let a host of Arsenal stars share their matchday experiences with you as you explore behind-the-scenes at Arsenal Football Club using audio visual guide handsets. You will explore areas such as the Directors Box, Home and Away Changing Rooms, Players Tunnel, Pitchside and more. All visits include FREE entry to the Arsenal Museum, branded Arsenal headphones and a tour certificate. Tickets are £20 per adult, £10 for children (under 16), with family tickets costing £50. Matchday tours and Legend Tours (held by ex-Arsenal players) are other options.

Stamford Bridge – Chelsea F.C.

Nearest Station: Fulham Broadway
Address: Fulham Road, London, SW6 1HS
Phone: 0207 386 9373
Website: www.chelseafc.com

Chelsea's Stadium, also known as Stamford Bridge, has a 41,798-seat capacity and is located in the affluent area of Fulham in central London.

Stamford Bridge offers a fantastic behind-the-scenes tour of the stadium at £19 per adult and £13 per child. The guided one-hour tour takes you behind the scenes, visiting various stands in the stadium, the press room, Home & Away dressing rooms, the tunnel and more.

All tours also include entry to the Museum, giving you the chance to see how Chelsea has evolved on and off the pitch to become one of the greatest football clubs in the world. The tours run daily (but not on match days and other dates – check online), and leave every 30 minutes from 10:00 to 15:00.

Museum-only admission is £11 per adult and £9 per child. Platinum tours, and legends tours are also available at an additional cost.

The Oval

Nearest Station: Oval
Address: The Oval, Kennington, London, SE11 5SS
Phone: 0844 375 1845
Website: www.kiaoval.com

The Oval Cricket Ground was built in 1845, and in 1880 hosted the first international test match between England and Australia. To this day, the final Test match of the English season is traditionally played here. The Oval has a seating capacity of 23,500.

The Oval was also the location of the first ever international football match in 1870 between England and Scotland.

Tours of the Oval are available. During the tour you will step foot in the players' dressing rooms, see where the players train, enter the press box, and access the Corinthian roof terrace with its stunning views of London. Tours take place on Saturdays at 11:00 on non-match days. Additional mid-week tour dates are available around key international fixtures. A full ground tour lasts approximately 90 minutes. Tickets are £15 per adult, £7.50 for children and concessions, with a family ticket costing £35. If booking in person, The Oval accepts cash only. Tickets may also be pre-booked online.

Twickenham Stadium

Nearest Station: Twickenham (National Rail)
Address: Whitton Road, Twickenham, TW2 7BA
Phone: 0871 222 2120
Website: www.englandrugby.com/twickenham/

Twickenham Stadium is the largest stadium in the world dedicated to rugby union, with a seating capacity of 82,000 people. Opened in 1909, it is mainly a rugby venue, but has also staged other events including mostly concerts from big names in the music industry like the Rolling Stones, The Police, Bon Jovi and Rihanna.

As well as rugby games themselves, tours are also offered at the stadium. Guided tours are priced at £20 per adult, £15 for concessions, £12 per child (5 to 15), and £50 for a family ticket. Included in the tour are the royal box, players' tunnel, a view of the arena from the top of the stand, and a pitchside walk, as well as a visit to the England dressing room where you will learn about the match-day preparations and routines of international rugby players. Tours also include entry to the World Rugby Museum.

Museum-only tickets are £8 for adults, £7 for concessions, £6 for children, and £25 for a family ticket. Stadium tours are not available on select dates due to matches and events at the stadium, so do check in advance before visiting. Museum entry on match days is only possible for match or event ticket holders. On Mondays, the museum is closed and tours do not run.

Wimbledon

Nearest Stations: Southfields and Wimbledon Park
Address: Church Road, Wimbledon, London, SW19 5AE
Phone: 0208 946 6131
Website: www.wimbledon.com

The best known and oldest Tennis tournament in the world, The Championships at Wimbledon should not be missed by any fans of the sport. Tickets for games are sold in advance through a ballot system whereby a computer randomly selects winners, and assigns them a game to watch. In 2016, The Championships run from 27th June to 10th July inclusive.

Wimbledon also runs tours and has a museum. More information on this is available in the neighbourhood guides section of this book, under "further afield".

Dining

London, as a booming city, boasts of an ever-evolving food scene that always keeps things fresh and exciting. In London, top hotels put in their best effort year after year to outdo each other by offering the tastiest afternoon teas, restaurants come up with inventive concepts to attract customers, and new chefs and kitchen talents are constantly emerging from all corners of the city.

If our dining recommendations in the neighbourhood guides were not enough to satisfy your cravings, there are even more in this section. Here we cover afternoon tea, luxury dining experiences, and affordable places to eat, giving you even more choices of where to dine.

Afternoon Tea

Afternoon tea, which is a common tradition today, owes its origins to Anna, the 7th Duchess of Bedford. In the 1800s, at a time when it was normal to eat only early morning breakfast and late evening dinner daily, Anna, irritated by the hunger each day as a result of no lunch, decided to take time out to take tea and snack each afternoon. Her daily practice was first done alone but over time, friends, relatives, associates and acquaintances followed suit, and the practice has become a tradition among the middle class today.

Afternoon tea is a charming, relaxing, tradition but in reality most Londoners do not have the time for this. However, almost everywhere you look in central London will offer this traditional delight. The practice is so famous in London that a "Tea Guild" exists that gives awards to hotels and tea rooms that offer the best tea services in the capital.

Where to go

According to the 2013 Tea Guild Awards, the best London Afternoon Tea spot is the prestigious **Goring Hotel** in Victoria *(Beeston Place, London, SW1W 0JW; 0207 396 9000; www.thegoring.com)*. Afternoon tea is served between 15:00 and 16:00 on weekdays, and 13:00 to 16:00 on Saturdays. Prices range from £42.50 to £62.50, depending on the package requested. Reservations are mandatory, and should be booked well in advance (usually up to 4 months) – even in low season you will find certain dates are fully booked.

Other notable and awarding-winning spots are:
* **Claridge's** *(Brook Street, London, W1K 4HR; 0207 629 8860; www.claridges.co.uk)* in Mayfair is one of the most famous locations for afternoon tea in London, with many arguing it is the best. Afternoon tea starts at £58 per person.
* **The Ritz** *(150 Piccadilly, London, E1J 9BR; 0207 493 8181; www.theritzlondon.com)* may well be known as the best location in London for afternoon tea, and was where The Queen Mother would come for hers. The quality, service and interiors of the building are simply stunning. Afternoon tea here begins at £52 per person.
* **Landmark Hotel** in Marylebone *(222 Marylebone Road, London, NW1 6JQ; 0207 631 8000; www.landmarklondon.co.uk)*, where the price for Afternoon tea starts at £45.
* **Bingham Hotel** in Richmond Upon Thames *(61-63 Petersham Road, Richmond, TW10 6UT; 020 8940 0902; www.thebingham.co.uk)*, is a boutique hotel outside of central London with views over the river. Afternoon here is just £25.
* **Browns Hotel** in Mayfair *(33 Albemarle Street, Mayfair, Greater London, W1S 4BP; 0207 493 6020; www.roccofortehotels.com)* serves afternoon tea with prices starting at £47.50. A Gluten Free Afternoon Tea is available here.
* **Four Seasons Hotel** just off Park Lane *(Hamilton Place, London W1J 7D; 0207 499 0888; www.fourseasons.com)* offers its afternoon tea from £39.
* **Capital Hotel** in Knightsbridge *(22-24 Basil Street, Knightsbridge, London, SW3 1AT; 0207 589 5171; www.capitalhotel.co.uk)*, serves traditional afternoon tea for £29.50, with a glass of champagne available for an extra £10.
* **Corinthia Hotel** by the Embankment and the river Thames *(Whitehall Place, London SW1A 2BD; 0207 930 8181; www.corinthia.com)* serves afternoon tea, starting at £50 per person.

The Savoy, The Montague on the Gardens, The Langham, The Anthenaeum, The Lanesborough, and **The Connaught** are other notable locations that offer wonderful afternoon tea experiences.

For all the above locations, reservations are either mandatory or highly recommended. A smart casual dress code applies to all locations. That means no shorts, sportswear, or cut off tank top-style vests; for most places a jacket and tie are optional for men. Jeans are also controversial. Tea times vary between locations, but you can generally find afternoon tea served between 14:00 and 17:00 daily.

Cheaper afternoon tea experiences

There are some bargain spots that offer afternoon tea for people who are on a budget. Places like the **National Portrait Gallery Restaurant**, offer great afternoon tea at the cost of £27.50, while the **Great Court Restaurant in the British Museum** goes for £19.50. **Kettner's** in Soho, offers tea at the rate of £24.95 while the Millbank Lounge (at the DoubleTree by Hilton London Westminster) goes for £21.95 per person.

Finally, two pubs in central London offer an affordable experience at about £11 in each – **The Cambridge** *(93 Charing Cross Road, London, WC2H 0DP; 0207 494 0338)*, and **The Wellington** in Covent Garden *(351 Strand, London, WC2R 0HS; 0207 836 2789)*. For the pubs, do call ahead to make sure afternoon tea is being offered on your visit date.

If you don't want the full afternoon tea experience, Cream Tea may be for you and offers a smaller portion size for a small price. Generally, Cream Tea omits the sandwiches included in the full afternoon tea experiences in favour of sweet bites such as scones. At the British Museum's Great Court Restaurant, for example, Cream Tea costs just £8.50.

Afternoon tea is here to stay and this culture will only be passed down from generation to generation, and is a rare, casual delight in such a bustling city.

Luxury Dining

The busy streets of London are replete with a plethora of bars and eateries, which serve all budgets. Some people prefer to keep to a budget set by the small pubs and market stalls in areas like Camden, whereas others prefer to splash the cash in bars and restaurants in the West End. Here we look at the upper end of the scale as we delve into the luxurious world of wining and dining in London.

Whether you are celebrating something special like a birthday, an engagement, an anniversary or just want to spoil yourself, London offers incredible culinary wizardry.

The city is home to a lot of impressive and innovative chefs and it has even been dubbed the culinary "Capital of the World". Below are some of our favourite luxury dining locations in London.

As with afternoon tea, a smart casual dress code applies. However, some locations do require that gentleman wear dinner jackets to enter. Reservations are strongly recommended at most locations; in some places they are mandatory. It is common practice for many high-end restaurants to add a 12.5% or 15% "discretionary" service charge to your bill. If you feel the service was not up to standard or you simply do not wish to pay it, you may ask for it to be removed as it is an optional extra.

Alain Ducasse at The Dorchester Hotel
(53 Park Lane, London, W1K 1QA; 0207 629 8866; **www.alainducasse-dorchester.com***)*
This three Michelin star restaurant headed by Chef Christophe Moret, offers top notch French cuisine and is a bit like stepping across the channel into France. The three-course a la carte menu starts at £95, four courses are £115, and a seven course tasting menu is £135. The lunch hour menu provides fantastic value, with a three-course meal including two glasses of wine priced at £60.

sketch – Lecture Room and Library
(9 Conduit Street, Mayfair, W1S 2XG; 0207 659 4500; **www.sketch.london***)*
A two Michelin star restaurant located in Mayfair, and partly owned by thirteen Michelin-starred chef, Pierre Gagnaire. Taster menus start from £81, while mains start at around £47. This is some of the most expensive food in London. The impressive wine list reaffirms the upscale nature of the restaurant, with wines prices all the way up to £17,000 a bottle.

L'Atelier de Joël Robuchon
(13-15 West Street, London, WC2H 9NE; 0207 010 8600;
www.joelrobuchon.co.uk)
This French restaurant, opened in 2006 by the renowned French chef Joël Robuchon, applies several French techniques to an affluent combination of ingredients from differing countries all over the world. This two Michelin star restaurant, offers meals that can easily top £200, as well as some more affordable options.

The 'Menu du Jour' offered at Lunch and pre-theatre is priced reasonably at £38 for three courses, and £43 for four courses. On the a la Carte menu mains are priced at £25 to £51, with Japanese Wagyusirloin steak going up to £53 per 100g. The five-course taster menu starts at £95, with eight courses from £129.

Restaurant Gordon Ramsay
(68 Royal Hospital Road, London, SW3 4HP; 0207 352 4441;
www.gordonramsayrestaurants.com/restaurant-gordon-ramsay)
This is one of only a couple of restaurants in London that holds three Michelin stars. The restaurant offers some of the best culinary encounters you are ever going to get in the country, and has been named the "Best Restaurant in the UK" on several occasions. A three course lunch menu is available for £65, with an all-day set menu available for £110. A seven-course Prestige Menu is £145.

Hibiscus
(29 Maddox Street, London, W1S 2PA; 0207 629 2999;
www.hibiscusrestaurant.co.uk)
This two Michelin starred restaurant in Mayfair has made it into the top ten spots of the United Kingdom Food guide. It is owned by Chef Claude Bosi and offers incredible delights.

The three-course set lunch menu is priced at £49.50. A 'surprise' tasting menu and a classics menu are both available for £135 a head. The restaurant sources indigenous British ingredients, including Cornish turbot and lamb from Somerset, through local suppliers.

Other luxury restaurants of note are **Le Gavroche**, **Hélène Darroze** at The Connaught, **The Greenhouse Restaurant**, **Marcus** at The Berkeley, and **Apsleys** at The Lanesborough.

Affordable Dining

London is a melting point for people from all financial backgrounds. From the ultra-rich to the not so well off. While life in the city may not be getting any cheaper, people's appetite for great value food has never been higher, and with the cost of travel and rent taking ever-growing chunks of people's salaries, finding the city's best budget restaurants is becoming more important than ever before. Here are some of our favourite, more affordable places to eat that are not fast-food chains.

Counter Café
(Pudding Mill Lane DLR Station; 7 Roach Road, London, E3 2PA; 0783 427 5920; www.counterproductive.co.uk/cafe)
The Counter Café, located at East London, offers views of the Olympic Stadium and deals on pies, brunches and salads. It offers a peaceful and quiet environment with a view of beautiful trees, the state of the art stadium and the small, local canal. Drinks and meals for two costs around £25, and other offers like homemade pies with salad cost £7, while Counter relish and bacon focaccia with eggs goes for £4.

101 Thai Kitchen
(Stamford Brook Station; 352 King Street, London, W6 0RX; 0208 746 6888; www.101thaikitchen.com)
Located in Haggerston, this joint produces real dishes with origins emanating from northern Thailand. Their green beans, garlic, stir-fried with chili, beef pad grape and holy basil costs £6.95, while a bowl of tom yum soup goes for £4.95. A meal for two with drinks costs around £35.

Bar Bruno
(Piccadilly Circus Station; 101 Wardour Street, London W1F 0UG; 0207 734 3750)
Located in Soho, one of London's most exclusive addresses, this place has been serving locals and visitors alike for decades. It serves delicious Italian food, as well as British classics, in large portions and may just be our favourite place for a budget meal in central London. £25 will easily get you a meal for two, with cash to spare.

Open from 6:00 to 22:00 daily, there is always something delicious to eat here all times of the day.

Wong Kei
(Piccadilly Circus Station; 41-43 Wardour Street, London, W1D 6PY; 0207 437 8408; www.wongkeilondon.com)

Until recently Wong Kei was known for its waiters' terrible attitudes – in our opinion it was the worst service in London – but this has gotten (slightly) better over recent years. It even became a bit of a tourist attraction in its own right because of its reputation. What is sure is that Wong Kei provides tasty Chinese dishes, huge portions and very low prices. A unique experience. Cash only.

There are a lot of other affordable diners in London and some of them include: **Canton Diner** in Chinatown, **The Clutch** in Haggerston, **Regency Café** in Kentish town, and **Tonkotsue East** in Soho.

Borough Market and Camden Market are the two definitive places to get fresh food from all around the world in minutes. The choice at both is huge and they are open for lunch year-round. Whether you fancy British, Portuguese, Indian, French, Jamaican or Chinese, there is something for everyone here.

Addresses for both markets are in the neighbourhood section of this guide.

Saving Money in London

London is without a doubt one of the most expensive cities in the world, but your visit to the city does not have to leave a hole in your pocket. Here are our top tips on how to save money.

1. Save money before you even get here – Flights and Accommodation
When making reservations for your flights, be sure to check both the official airline websites, as well as travel brokers. Websites like **www.expedia.com**, **www.skyscanner.net** and **www.kayak.com** search many flights sellers at once. Will having a stopover, for example, save you hundreds of pounds? Or changing your arrival or departure airport?

The place you stay will have a big effect on how much you spend on your trip to London, especially if your stay is longer than a few days. The following few questions are important: How central do you want to stay? What amenities do you realistically need? Are you loyal to a certain brand?

Once you have answered those, go on to a hotel comparison website such as **www.hotels.com**, **www.expedia.com** or **www.booking.com**. Use all of these, plus any others you know, to get the best deal. The same hotel will often be available through different websites for the different prices, and sometimes the savings can be substantial. If you have loyalty points to use, why not use those?

Do you need a luxury hotel or will a budget chain like a TravelLodge, Holiday Inn, or EasyHotel do? If you can stay in a budget chain, the savings can be huge. Other affordable chains include Novotel, Ibis Budget and Premier Inn.

Airbnb.com is another option for travelers, where you can rent out a room in someone's house, or even an entire apartment. Although you are not necessarily going to pay less money overall, you may be able to find a nicer apartment that more closely mirrors London life for a similar price for a hotel room. If you are going to be touring for more than a week, this is a good option to stay in a more residential neighborhood, as opposed to only being amongst tourists. It also allows you to cook your own meals, saving a bit of money there too.

Lastly, there is couch surfing – a free, or minimal cost opportunity – orchestrated online to, quite literally, crash on someone's couch. While this may be a viable option, one thing to note is that space is perceived very differently by Londoners than most other people. Londoners are used to less space than many people around the world. If you need a lot of privacy and quiet, this is probably not the best option.

Finally, get travel insurance before leaving home, so if you have a problem you will be covered. This may increase the cost of your trip by a little bit, but will save you a lot of money if something goes wrong.

2. Arriving in London
Once you have hopped off the plane, you need to make your way to your accommodation, do you need a taxi to get you there? Or will a train or bus be cheaper, and possibly even quicker? Pre-book your train tickets to save money too. For large groups, public transport may work out more expensive than the equivalent journey in a cab.

3. Vouchers and Coupons
Restaurants, attractions and even shops want to compete for your custom. Look out online for vouchers and coupons which can save you a bit of money. You may also find these in leaflets at hotels and tourist information centres. Whether it is a percentage off, or a set amount of money, it all adds up over your trip to London.

4. Attractions and Museums
First of all, make a list of the attractions you want to see before visiting. Most cultural attractions and museums are free admission in London, which is fantastic.

Secondly, for paid attractions, visit the attraction's website and pre-purchase your tickets online. This can save you a substantial amount of money over the 'on the day' gate price.

Be sure to check whether attractions have partnered with each other too, or whether they are part of the same company. Partnered attractions usually offer ticket combo deals where you purchase tickets for several attractions at once at a discount price. A good example are all the attractions in London operated by Merlin Entertainments such as the London Eye, London Dungeon, London Aquarium, Madame Tussauds, and Shrek's Adventure – you can get combo tickets for all of these and save up to 40%.

5. Save BIG money on attractions by 'travelling by train'

Here is one of our favourite tips – and a big secret. National Rail offers a "Days Out" promotion with 2 for 1 deals on a huge number of major London attractions. This involves you travelling by rail to London in order to get the discount.

If you are already in London, however, you can get around this. First of all, visit **www.daysoutguide.co.uk** and browse the offers available and print out vouchers for any attractions you wish to visit.

Then, simply visit any London National Rail Station (note: not the Underground stations, but National Rail) such as Waterloo, King's Cross, St. Pancras, London Bridge, etc. Go to a ticket machine and purchase a cheap ticket from anywhere with London as the destination – get the cheapest ticket possible. Usually there will be one for a few pounds. Once you have your ticket, there is no need to use it but do keep it safe.

Then, simply present your train ticket with your printed voucher at your chosen attraction's entrance and you will get 2 for 1 entry. This works on major attractions such as The Tower of London, London Eye, Madame Tussauds, Thames Clippers, Hampton Court Palace, and many other attractions covered in this book.

6. Consider a London Pass

If you think you will be visiting a lot of London attractions, consider getting a London Pass – this is a one-fee pass that includes entry into many of London's major attractions and tours, with over sixty included. It even includes a one-day hop-on, hop-off bus ticket on Golden Tours.

Note that none of the Merlin Entertainment attractions are included in the London Pass (the London Eye, London Dungeon, London Aquarium, Shrek's Adventure and Madame Tussauds), and neither is The Shard. Some attractions will grant you express entry with the London Pass. Adult prices are £59 for one day, £79 for 2 days, £95 for 3 days and £129 for 6 days. Child prices are at least £20 cheaper. We advise against getting the Travelcard add-on as this works out more expensive than paying for transport yourself separately.

7. Getting around London

If using public transport within London, get an Oyster Card or use a contactless payment card for the best value.

If you are only staying in central London, consider travelling by bus only instead of the Undergound. This way, the most you will ever spend on transport is £4.50 per day.

If you were planning on using taxis a lot, use the Underground instead. Or if you want the privacy, use ride-sharing service Uber is a cheaper alternative to the black London cabs.

8. London Tours

Hop On, Hop Off bus tours are a great way to understand the layout of the city and learn about its history. However, we would not use them to get between attractions due to their often indirect routes. Once you have understood where everything is, and have enjoyed the commentary, it is time to swap to public transport to make the most of your time in London.

Big Bus Tours, Original Sightseeing Tours, Golden Tours and London City Tour are the four big operators. The first two listed are the biggest. Haggle with ticket agents to get the best price, and purchase the shortest ticket length (generally 24 hours). Although the second day may "only be £5 more", the tube and London Buses can get you around for a similar price and much more quickly.

Many of these companies sell their tickets as 24, 48 and 72-hour tickets. However, you should be aware that 24-hour tickets are not really 24-hours as the last tours usually depart between 16:30 and 19:00 depending on the season. The 12-hours they are shut for service are mysteriously rarely mentioned.

Ticket agents can also get you discounted attraction tickets once you have a bus tour ticket.

Alternatively, there are literally hundreds of walking tour companies out there offering all variety of tours. If you are unsure, then consider one of two free walking tour companies out there – FreeToursByFoot.com and FreeLondonWalkingTours.com – both are excellent and allow you to choose your own price per tour after you have taken them. We recommend £5 to £10 per person as a good benchmark for a two-hour tour.

9. Save money when shopping

London is renowned for its wealth of luxury shopping, but there are also fantastic bargains to be had. Crucially, remember to shop around. What may be £40 in one shop, may just be £25 further down the road.

If you are around after Christmas, the Boxing Day sales start on 26th December each year. On Boxing Day shoppers usually begin queuing up outside big London stores before the sun rises to get the best bargains as soon as the shops open. If you are not that keen, just keep an eye out for the sales signs throughout your trip.

10. Save on Theatre Tickets

A trip to London would not be complete without taking in a West End show. However, these can be very expensive, with the priciest seats regularly selling for upwards of £65 each.

You should be aware that most theatres have more affordable ticket options available for each show, with the cheapest seats usually available from £15.

Most theatres also offer 'day seats' that are usually the front row – these are sold daily at the theatres' box office opening time for shows showing the same day. These are usually very well priced (£30 maximum), though not everyone may appreciate being that close to the stage.

TKTS, located in Leicester Square, is another fantastic option. Open year-round, this theatre ticket booth is the official seller of tickets for all of London's shows. Plus, you can save up to 50% on shows if you buy the tickets on the day of performance. Check their website at **www.tkts.co.uk** to see which tickets are on sale today, tomorrow and later in the week, as well as their prices.

You will also see other discounted theatre booths in central London, particularly around Piccadilly Circus and Leicester Square. Check their authenticity, and if it all checks out, you could save a lot of money.

Finally, a couple of times a year, the theatres all club together for discounted theatre events, with tickets available for almost every show. In January and February each year, **www.getintolondontheatre.co.uk** offers amazing deals from just £10 on big shows, whereas **www.kidsweek.co.uk** offers 'kids go free' deals to shows every August (up to the age of 16). These tickets must be pre-booked online and carry no booking fees.

2016 Seasonal Events

London always has something interesting and different going on whenever you visit. Here is a month by month list of some the events throughout the year.

January
New Year's Day Parade

1st January 2016
Over 10,000 performers take to the streets of London on New Year's Day to celebrate in style. Having been performed yearly since 1987, this is now a big international event with over 600,000 spectators present every year and a TV audience of over 300 million worldwide.

The parade route usually starts in Berkley Street (by Green Park), makes its way up to Piccadilly Circus, turns down Haymarket, goes around Trafalgar Square, down Whitehall, and ends in Parliament Square by Big Ben and the Houses of Parliament. Admission is free. Local roads around the parade route are usually closed to traffic from 04:00 to 18:00 on this day.

February
Chinese New Year
14th February 2016
Although Chinese New Year itself is on the 8th February in 2016, the celebrations will be held on the subsequent weekend. You can celebrate the start of the Year of the Monkey all around the West End with events held on Trafalgar Square and Chinatown from 10:00 to 18:00. London's Chinese New Year celebrations are the largest outside Asia, with parades, performances and fireworks.

At 10:00 a large lion parade makes its way from Trafalgar Square to Chinatown; from 12:00 onwards stage performances are held; and at 17:20 the grand finale begins as dancers and acrobats take to the stage, and pyrotechnics illuminate Nelson's Column.

March
St. Patrick's Day Celebrations
13th March 2016
Although, St. Patrick's Day is on the 17th March each year, it is traditional for the large celebrations in London to be held on a Sunday. The day celebrates one of the patron Saints of Ireland, and is a national holiday in that country.

This year, Sunday 13th March will be the big St Patrick's Day Parade in London, with floats, marching bands from across the UK, sports clubs and Irish dancing schools. The London St Patrick's Day Parade follows the same route as the aforementioned New Year's Day Parade.

On Trafalgar Square, there will be Irish food on sale, as well as music and traditional dancing. There is also usually a whole host of children's activities.

Boat Races

19th March 2016 and 27th March 2016
Two different boat races take place along a 4.25-mile (6.8km) stretch of the river Thames. The "Head of the River Race" takes place at 13:30 on 19th March 2016 from Mortlake to Putney. Over 400 crews of eights take part, making it one of the highest participation events in London. The race was first held in 1926.

The Oxford and Cambridge Races are perhaps more well-known, and race the same route but in the opposite direction – from Putney to Mortlake. In 2016 the event takes place on 27th March. The first race took place in 1829 in Henley on Thames, following a challenge between old school friends.

The best place to watch the event is from one of the many pubs that line this section of the river. Admission is free.

April
St. George's Day Celebrations
2016 date to be confirmed
St. George, the patron Saint of England, is celebrated every year in Trafalgar Square. The event is free to attend and usually involves food stalls serving traditional English fare, free activities and shows, and activities for kids too.

St. George's Day is celebrated on April 23rd in 2016, but dates for the annual celebration on Trafalgar Square have not yet been revealed. In our opinion either the 23rd or 24th are safe bets, however.

London Marathon

24th April 2016
Whether you fancy running yourself, or watching and supporting others, the London Marathon will get you into the running spirit. The marathon takes place all over central, east and south London with major road closures all across the city from approximately 07:00 to 19:00.

Charges apply to enter the Marathon. Running places are balloted and this year they sold out over 6 months in advance. Spectators do not need a ticket.

May
Museums at Night
11th to 14th May 2016

Museums at Night is where several museums, galleries and heritage sites throughout the UK throw open their doors after hours to showcase their treasures in unexpected ways. Museums participating in the May event that have announced participation at the time of writing include: London Museum of Water and Steam, Horniman Museum and Gardens, and Banqueting House. More museums will be announced closer to the event date. More information is available at **www.museumsatnight.org.uk**.

The event returns for a second time later in the year on 28th and 29th October 2016.

The RHS Chelsea Flower Show

24th to 28th May

The Chelsea Flower Show has been held in the grounds of the Royal Hospital Chelsea, London every year since 1913. It is an extremely popular event where designers, local councils and individuals compete to design the most beautiful and interesting garden.

With over 150,000 visitors each year, tickets must be purchased in advance due to the limited capacity at the event grounds.

Innovative winning gardens in recent years include James May's garden made entirely of plasticine, and Diarmuid Gavin's Irish Sky Garden, the first garden to be suspended in the air.

June
Queen's Birthday Celebrations
10th to 12th June 2016

2016 is a big year for Britain, as Queen Elizabeth II reaches the age of 90. Although her actual birthday is on 21st April, we celebrate it in the summer due to the likelihood of better weather.

The celebrations will begin with a service of Thanksgiving at St Paul's Cathedral on Friday 10th June, which marks the Duke of Edinburgh's 95th birthday, as well as the start of Her Majesty's official birthday weekend.

The next day, 11th June, will be the official birthday of The Queen, with her family members joining her for the traditional Trooping the Colour parade between Buckingham Palace and Horse Guards Parade. The royal family will also gather on the balcony at Buckingham Palace for a fly-past by the Royal Air Force.

Finally, on 12th June The Patron's Lunch will take place – a ticketed event open to the public (tickets from £150) – on The Mall which is being called the "biggest street party" the nation has ever seen, with 10,000 people in attendance.

West End Live
18th and 19th June 2016

This free annual event showcases the best of the West End in Trafalgar Square. All day Saturday and Sunday you can turn up and see what's on. On stage, the casts of some of London's most well-known shows will be performing live numbers.

Eateries, small shops and kids' activities round out this family friendly event. This is a great way to sample a selection of West End shows, and then purchase tickets to the one(s) you enjoy most.

Pride in London Festival
25th June 2016

The Pride in London festival, a celebration of the lesbian, gay, bisexual and transgender (LGBT+) community across London as an event continues to increase in size year after year.

Performances, speeches and other forms of art will take place throughout the week at various locations around London running from 18th to 26th June. The culmination of the festival, however, is the large scale Pride in London Parade which this year takes place on the 25th June. It will travel all the way from Baker Street down to Trafalgar Square. Then, throughout the day speeches and performances adorn the square's stage.

July
BBC Proms

15th July to 10th September 2016
This classic musical festival, hosted by the BBC at the Royal Albert Hall, is a delight to attend. With standing tickets only costing £5 each, the aim is to bring live classical music within the reach of all. Tickets for seats start at £16.

On the last night of the show, as so many people want to see the finale, the solution has been to set up giant screens – dubbed Proms in the Park – which allow you to watch the same spectacle, but outdoors in Hyde Park.

August
Prudential Ride London
30th and 31st July 2016
Developed by the Mayor of London and his agencies, Prudential Ride London is a world-class festival of cycling.

For anyone wanting to take part, FreeCycle is a 10-mile track around central London's famous landmarks with roads closed to vehicles, making them free from traffic. You can join the route at any point, do as many laps as you like and come and go as you please.

Cyclists can stop off en route to enjoy a range of bike-based entertainment and activities all around central London. You can either sign up in advance for some goodies, or turn up on the day. This takes place on the 30th July.

As well as that, the four different competitive races will take place over the course of the weekend; some races span up to 200km in length! A Cycling Show will also take place in East London at the Excel Centre from 28th to 30th July 2016.

Notting Hill Carnival

28th and 29th August 2016
Each year in August, Notting Hill is home to the world's second-biggest carnival – Notting Hill Carnival – where London's West Indian communities gather to put on a street festival that is a joy to experience, and is filled with fantastic photo opportunities.

From the colourful costumes and floats on the main parade, to the Caribbean food and live music, this event is a huge amount of fun, with people from all backgrounds celebrating together.

September
Open House Weekend London
17th and 18th September 2016
Having started in 1992, Open House Weekend was created to open up London's incredible buildings to the general public who don't otherwise have access. Today, it has grown in popularity with dozens of locations participating. It is as much about looking at historic buildings, as it is about master planning and a look towards the future.

Buildings and areas open to the public in 2015 included Burlington House's many areas, the Temple area, Fitzrovia Chapel, the Farringdon Crossrail construction site, the Royal College of Physicians, and more.

London Design Festival
17th to 25th September 2016

This annual art and design festival is a fantastic opportunity to see works from both established and up-and-coming artists. The festival is not confined to one area of London, but rather has several events throughout the city. In 2015, the event was centered around the V&A Museum and Somerset House, and we expect this to once again be the case in 2016.

Exact details on the exhibitions and installations on show were not available at the time of writing, but be sure to check **www.londondesignfestival.com** for more information closer to the festival start dates.

October
Diwali: Festival of Lights at Trafalgar Square

2016 date to be confirmed

Diwali, also known as the Festival of Lights, is an event which celebrates the triumph of light over dark, and good over evil. The festival is very popular in certain Asian countries but is now celebrated by people of all faiths and nationalities in London.

Diwali on Trafalgar Square includes a children's parade, live performances throughout the day, eateries and more.

The 2016 date for the event has not yet been revealed. More information will be available closer to the time at **www.diwaliinlondon.com**.

Frieze London
6th to 9th October 2016
October is another great month for art lovers, as the world-renowned Frieze London event is held. This ticketed event allows you to see contemporary art in Regent's Park. The 2015 edition of the festival included works from 164 galleries from 27 countries. The 2016 event is expected to be even bigger.

More information on 2016 exhibitors and ticket prices will be available closer to the festival start date at **www.friezelondon.com**.

November
Christmas Lights Switch On
2016 dates to be confirmed
London gets into the Christmas spirit quite early in the year, as the Christmas Lights along Oxford Street and Regent Street are turned on a full 6 to 8 weeks before Christmas Day.

Both the events are popular and free to attend, and take place on different days. You can expect live music and entertainment, and usually a celebrity appearance to turn the lights on. After the switch on event, the lights stay on continuously until early January.

In 2015, the Oxford Street lights were switched on 1st November by Kylie Minogue, and Regent Street's ceremony took place on 15th November. Exact dates and details are usually announced in October each year.

Bonfire Night
5th November 2016
Bonfire Night is a celebration of the failed plot to blow up Parliament in 1605. Guy Fawkes, a member of the Gunpowder Plot, placed explosives under the House of Lords in order to assassinate King James I. The plot was foiled, and to remember this each year on 5th November an annual celebration is held all across the UK. The event usually involves burning an effigy of Guy Fawkes, as well as a large fireworks display.

There are many fireworks displays in London on this night run by local councils. Firework displays can usually be found in Blackheath, Wimbledon Park, Southwark Park, Cleveland Square in Westminster, and many others further out of central London.
Many of these ask for a small entrance fee or a donation. Others require you to pre-book entry tickets in advance.

Winter Wonderland London

Late November 2016 to Early January 2017

Located on the Park Lane side of Hyde Park, Winter Wonderland is one of the go-to places during the Christmas season each year. It is a huge well-themed, funfair style attraction.

Admission into Winter Wonderland is free, with activities and food charged individually. Rides are one of the staples of the funfair with everything from ghost trains to helter-skelters, and even a giant Ferris wheel. There are also all manner of shops to buy Christmas themed merchandise, beer tents are also a common staple of the event, as are a host of places to eat. It is good family fun and worth visiting.

Opening times are usually 10:00 to 22:00 daily. Closed on Christmas Day. 2016 dates for the event had not been announced at the time of writing.

December
Great Christmas Pudding Race
3rd December 2016

Taking place in Covent Garden, this 35-year-old tradition is a charity event, which sees people trying to complete an obstacle course in the quickest time possible.

The catch is that each contestant must carry a Christmas pudding round the course and get it back in perfect condition. This is all done while going up and down slides, through slaloms, and more. Great fun to watch.

In 2015 the event took place on 5th December. 2016 dates were not available at the time of writing.

New Year's Eve

31st December 2016

London does New Year's Eve in style with firework displays all across town. The big one, however, is the Mayor of London's fireworks on the River Thames and the London Eye. Year after year, these fireworks have amazed Londoners and visitors alike, and they are even timed to music.

This is an extremely popular event; tickets for viewing areas are required and are available at £10 each. There are also views of the fireworks from non-ticketed areas and also from further afield but these are less than ideal. Even with a ticket, count on getting there quite a few hours early for the best spots.

A Special Thanks!

If you have made it this far, thank you very much for reading everything. We hope this guide will make a big difference to your trip to London! Remember to take this guide with you whilst you are visiting this amazing city.

You may be interested to know that Independent Guides runs tours of London held by the author of this book. These can be completely customised to your needs. Multi-day discounts are available, as are group discounts. Tours are tailor-made to your specification. We guarantee an unforgettable tailor-made visit to London. Contact us directly via the link below, and we will work together.

If you have any questions or wish to contact us (including for guided tour bookings), you can do so using the form at **www.independentguidebooks.com/contact-us/**. If you have any corrections, feedback about any element of the guide, or a review of an attraction, hotel, area or restaurant – send us a message and we will get back to you.

We also encourage you to leave a review on the Amazon website, or wherever you have purchased this guide from. Your reviews make a huge difference in helping other people find this guide, and we really appreciate your help.

If you have enjoyed this guide, other travel guides in this series include:
* **The Independent Guide to New York City**
* **The Independent Guide to Paris**
* **The Independent Guide to Orlando**
* **The Independent Guide to Universal Orlando**
* **The Independent Guide to Disneyland**
* **The Independent Guide to Disneyland Paris**
* **The Independent Guide to Walt Disney World**
* **The Independent Guide to Universal Studios Hollywood**

Have a fantastic time in London!

Photo Credits:

Front Cover credits: Houses of Parliament – Martin Hesketh, Tower Bridge – Tony Smith, Guards – Gabriel Villena,

Inside photo credits: British Museum – Rick Harris; The Royal Mews – 'Laika ac'; The Jewel Tower – David Holt; St. James's Palace – Roland Turner; Horse Guards Parade – Loco Steve; Churchill War Rooms – 'Tracey & Doug'; Heathrow – eGuide Travel; Eurostar – Loco Steve; Ferry – Roel Hemkes; People of London – Andy Roberts; Oyster Card – Amanda Slater; red London bus – Metro Centric; DLR – George Rex; Santander Cycles and London Canal Museum – Elliott Brown; Thames Clippers boat (also used on cover) – Matt Buck; Westminster Abbey – Judy Dean; Tate Britain – morebyless; The Cenotaph – Foreign and Commonwealth Office; Trafalgar Square – Christian Reimer; National Portrait Gallery – David Holt; London Transport Museum – © TfL, from London Transport Museum Collection; Somerset House – Lars Ploughmann; Royal Courts of Justice – Ronnie Macdonald; Cleopatra's Needle – Charles D P Miller; Brompton Oratory – Tony Hisgett; Saatchi Gallery and Middle Temple – Jim Linwood; Museum of London – Ewa Munro; St. Paul's Cathedral – Loco Steve; Fleet Street Dragon – Loz Pycock; Guildhall Art Gallery – Elias Gayles; Tate Modern – Chris Sampson; Shakespeare's Globe – Tom Bastin; Regent's Park – Paul Hudson; London Zoo – Kent Wang; Madame Tussauds – Karen Roe; Sherlock Holmes Museum – Anders Rasmussen; The Wallace Collection – Megan Eaves; Kew Gardens – Russell Bowes; Richmond Park – 'Jack'; Warner Bros Studio Tour and Legoland Windsor – Gary Bembridge; Hampton Court Palace – Amanda Slater; Wimbledon – Phil Whitehouse; Windsor Castle – Jean-Marc Astesana; Banqueting House – www.traveljunction.com; Westminster Cathedral – Andrew Gray; Battle of Britain London Memorial – David Holt; Imperial War Museum – Ann Lee; Ripley's – Ben Sutherland; Borough Market – Magnus D; Oxford Street – Andrew Nash; Westfield – Jim Linwood; Piccadilly and Lord's Cricket Ground – 'Dncnh'; Brick Lane – Garry Knight; Bicester Village – Neil Turner; Dominion Theatre Interior – Mario Sánchez Prada; Wembley Arena – Vinqui; Southbank Centre – Matt Brown; Wembley Stadium – Lee Thomas; Emirates Stadium – Llyod Morgan; Stamford Bridge – Jason Bagley; The Oval – Welivecricket.com; Twickenham Stadium – Marco Poggiaroni; Afternoon tea – Connie Ma; New Year's Day Parade, Pudding Race and Notting Hill Carnival – S Pahkrin; Chinese New Year – Paul; Boat Races – Robbie Shade; London Marathon – Malcolm Murdoch; Chelsea Flower Show – Karen Roe; BBC Proms – Yuichi Shiraishi; Diwali and Winter Wonderland – Garry Knight; and New Year's Fireworks – Natesh Ramasamy

Maps provided by OpenStreetMap.

Printed in Great Britain
by Amazon